September '82

S×

for sharing
rience of Maui

Vicki E.
Rocki

MAUI
No Ka Oi

This is Maui. Dawn at Ke'anae, on the rugged Hana shore, reflects the island and the young population of Maui. A new kind of people on this earth, building and living in a unique island community that surely must be the envy of the world.

Wailuku, political center of Maui and a jumble of old and new, spreads awkwardly across the entrance to 'Iao Valley. Within the round valley a famous tourist landmark, 'Iao Needle, identifies the eroded knife edge of a narrow ridge, remnant of an extinct volcano comprising West Maui.

▷ Overleaf. Introduced from South Africa and Ethiopia, Protea are the newest exotic introduction to Maui's festival of people and flowers. Growing high on the Kula slopes are the Duchess Protea, two Frosted Wine Banksia, and a white Ric-Rac Banksia. Opposite, the pink Rainbow Shower tree is a native of Central America.

Maui is four islands floating in the sun, and two, Lana'i and Moloka'i, are of the kind that urban dwellers dream. The Lana'ihale forest, hidden in a seemingly perpetual fog, is seen only by those willing to walk in the rain. Moloka'i's north pali at sunset is seen only by campers willing to swim through the surf for a place on the beach at Wailau.

◇Overleaf. Another introduction to Maui during the last decade is the condominium landscape. Along the beach shore at Wailea is a tropical environment for living created with water and palms from sand dunes and kiawe by Maui's oldest kama'aina corporation, Alexander & Baldwin, Inc.

The famous Hana Road. Not a road to go anywhere on—the Hana Road is a destination in itself. It winds some fifty miles, beginning at funky Paia town, into and out of narrow valleys and under tropical forests. The road is completely hidden at Honomanu Bay pali under a mixed forest canopy of orange African tulip blossoms, coconut palms, blossoming mango and pale-leaved indigenous kukui trees. The Hawaii taro-leaf-shaped road sign identifies the highway beyond Hana town, where pea vine only partly reveals the sign—to the concerned environmentalist a proper way to maintain the scenic highways of Maui.

Maui island displays a constantly changing panorama of natural beauty and people, all sharing an amazingly diversified island landscape, which is typified by the dry sandy beach and kiawe of Wailea and the contrasting wet mountains and cane fields of West Maui. Sugarcane keeps the land green where golf courses and rain do not. Visitors and residents crowded together by zoning restrictions and sun along the west shore keep the rest of Maui Island the way it's always been.

The smallest island of Maui County is tiny Molokini, a partially drowned volcanic crater. The summit rain forest on Lana'i Island shares its wet habitat with Norfolk Island pines from the southern hemisphere and indigenous ohi'a lehua trees and ferns that have always lived in Hawaii.

All of this is Maui
A land found in the ocean,
Thrown up out of the sea,
From the very depths of Kanaloa,
The white coral in the watery caves
That caught on the hook of the fisherman,
The great fisherman of Kapaahu,
The great fisherman, Kapuheʻeuanuʻu . . .
                    —chant of Makuakaumana.

MAUI
No Ka Oi

Text and Photography by

ROBERT WENKAM

A Wenkam / Candère Book

 Rand McNally & Company · Chicago · New York · San Francisco

Acknowledgements

It is easy to research, write, and photograph a beautiful island, but difficult and expensive to combine the words and pictures into a large-format book like *Maui No Ka Oi.* Alexander & Baldwin, Inc., the kama'aina corporation that helped Maui get started, provided the financial grant necessary to get me started and made possible the book of this size and quality. Working with the people at A&B has made *Maui No Ka Oi* a far better book than otherwise possible.

Hospitality has been most enjoyable with Calvin and Lee Wilson in Ka'anapali, Ed and Fran Pattimore on Lana'i, and Dr. and Mrs. Milton Howell and John Elliott in Hana. It has been most informative to talk with Jim Luckey at the Lahaina Restoration Foundation; Sharon Lawrence, owner of the Blue Max; Kenneth Emory and E.H. Bryan, Jr., at the Bishop Museum in Honolulu; Abe Piianaia of the University of Hawaii Hawaiian Studies Program; Lt. Jamie Davidson of the U.S. Navy, who arranged for me to visit Kaho'olawe as working press; Pardee Erdman, owner of 'Ulupalakua Ranch; the reference room at the Skokie Public Library in Illinois and the fine facilities at the Kahului Public Library on Maui; design advice from Neal Carlson in Chicago; flower and Protea information from Philip Parvin of the University of Hawaii Maui Agricultural Research Center in Kula; and one of the very important people in writing a book, Claire Gosly, who did the typing; and many others with whom I met and chatted briefly on the Maui islands. I should also mention the A&B company magazine, *Ampersand,* and *The Lanaian,* a monthly newspaper produced by the Lana'i Community Services Council. And I thank Maui for being such a great island to photograph and write of, and the Hawaiian people on Kaho'olawe for their concern and Aloha 'aina.

R. Wenkam

Other books with photographs and text by Robert Wenkam:
The Garden Island Kauai • Honolulu Is An Island
The Big Island Hawaii • New England • Hawaii
Maui: The Last Hawaiian Place
Micronesia Island Wilderness (with Kenneth Brower)
Micronesia Breadfruit Revolution (with Byron Baker)

Editor • Herb Luthin, Chicago
Sketches • Tad Wenkam
Design and layout • Robert Wenkam, Honolulu
Production • Wenkam/Candere, Honolulu
Composition • The Composing Room, Irvine
Color Separations • Color Graphics, San Diego
Printing • Kingsport Press, Kingsport
Photographs • Canon AE-1, Kodachrome 64

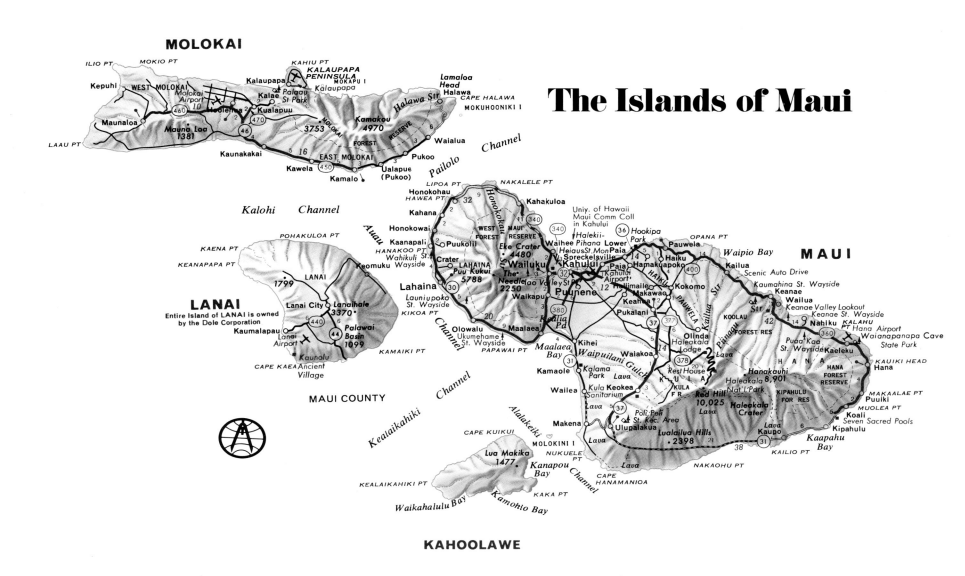

The Islands of Maui

Contents

I grew up with Maui, beginning when Maui was a very different island. I've watched thirty-five years of changes as Maui evolved from a rural island of cows, cane, and pineapple into a cosmopolitan tourist-oriented community that still has space for cows, cane, and pineapple, but has added condominiums, continental restaurants, and hotels. Most of this new building has occurred in the leeward coastal areas where the climate is best for living, so the magnificent scenery and vast upland wilderness of Maui remain relatively untouched while alternative rural lifestyles and opportunities for luxury condominiums are enhanced. Oldtime Maui residents, new apartment dwellers, and casual tourists are all beneficiaries of a new kind of island living. Only the adverse consequences of uncontrolled increases in residential and tourist populations are cause for concern to an island looking forward to a bright future, for Maui, in many respects, may be a better place to live today than thirty-five years ago when I first arrived.

Maui was disgorged from the sea in a great volcanic eruption as the earth's crust slid slowly across a hot crack in the ocean floor; early Hawaii ali'i described the beginnings in much the same way as contemporary plate tectonics. Dormant Haleakala last erupted about 1790.

Haleakala's crater is 3,000 feet deep, and 21 miles in circumference. Chicago's Sears Tower would be hidden behind the 1,000-foot-high cinder cones. On the outer slope, the southwest rift cinder cones are green in the deep pasture grass of 'Ulupalakua Ranch.

Overleaf. Between lofty Haleakala and the much lower West Maui Mountains, lie the flat plains of central Maui. Before sugar became Maui's dominant agricultural crop, the Wailuku plains were drifting sand dunes, with dust blown on the high winds generated by a funneling venturi effect of the two mountain masses. Alexander & Baldwin's century-old-irrigation system brings water from the windward side of Maui via 70 miles of tunnels and ditches, to the once arid valley into an always green carpet of sugar cane. Across from West Maui, the winding road above Kula climbs it's twisting way upward, to the summit of Haleakala, with a panoramic vista of central Maui at every turn.

Magenta ti blossoms emulate the great rainbow arc of an afternoon rain shower drifting across Kula rangelands. From Makawao and Hai'ku, squalls wet the dry pastures of Haleakala Ranch.

The sharply eroded summit of Puʻu Kukui, shrouded by clouds during every tradewind afternoon and sparkling clear again in the morning, is evocative of the drama and mystique of a changeable island environment. At dawn Maui is suspended on the sea, and reflected in the unruffled waters of Kupeke, an ancient Hawaii fishpond on Molokai.

Lana'i Island is always floating offshore: south of Moloka'i, west of Maui, north of Kaho'olawe. It is the backdrop to a variety of stage happenings, whether on crowded Front Street in Lahaina with visiting yachts inshore, or fragrant, dazzling flower farms of the Kula highlands. It is where the sun goes down . . . the final curtain to a Maui day.

Maui girl—a new generation. As beautiful as the island where she lives.

1

Maui: The Last Place on Earth

This is the story of astounding ocean voyages and the creation of lost civilizations, of incredible people of three worlds, of pioneering sugar planters and a gambling King of Hawaii. Of the very early years, any accounting is mostly conjecture and deduction—wooden boats and thatched huts left no archaeological evidence. In later years, the ocean people without written records made it necessary to record oral history and to view dances to reveal historical trails. These are the threads of history woven into a tapestry of people and events, combining known facts with an understanding of what must have happened.

> But, after all, who knows, and who can say
> whence it all came, and how creation happened?
> The gods themselves are later than creation,
> so who knows truly whence it has arisen?
> Whence all creation had its origin,
> he, whether he fashioned it or whether he did not,
> he, who surveys it all from highest heaven,
> he knows—or maybe even he does not know.

> —The Hymn of Creation from the *Rig Veda* (x-129).

They were like us. They thought of what it was like on the other side of the mountain—or in the next valley. They were innovative and solved problems. Smaller in stature and less muscular than earlier primitive people, their larger brain capacity, compared with Java and Peking man, enabled these new people to accomplish things that brawn alone had never done.

The earliest of people hunted and gathered food in Africa, Europe, and Asia, hundreds of thousands of years ago. They scratched and painted pictures of wild animals in their cave shelters—then died out. Possibly from lack of food, or not knowing how to grow it; from the cold of advancing glacial ice; from being isolated in tribal groups too small to reproduce and thrive. Or perhaps, like animals, an interest in living did not exist. There was no need to live.

It would be too incredible to conclude that people like us sprang into life independently and simultaneously in many parts of the world, "fully formed as from the brow of Zeus." We must have first evolved in one place and then migrated to different parts of the earth, as our developing skills enabled us to utilize the products of the earth and respond advantageously to changing environmental events. When the rain, sun, and wind were no longer to be feared—but were to be used.

As the northern glacial ice shield started to melt, marking the end of the last great ice epoch, weather patterns changed around the globe. And the oceans, nearly 300 feet below their present level, began rising, forcing those living along the shores to abandon their huts and move to a new living place, just as the Polynesians were to do many years later when they departed Tahiti, sailing away to a new island home in Hawaii. The story of Maui begins when these first ocean travelers, on a continent far away, began their long voyage eastward, perhaps 100,000 years ago.

As glacial ice continued to retreat during several hundred years, fishermen working eastern shore beaches of the African continent began venturing northward along the uninhabited coastline, looking for better fishing opportunities, but returning home before sundown. Later women and men fished together on longer trips, too distant to return by nightfall. Perhaps they extended visits to a particularly bountiful and sheltered bay for weeks or more. Some never returned. They stayed and established new communities like their successors would do for tens of thousands of years to come. When adverse weather halted the more adventurous sailors in their fragile boats, and primitive agricultural methods failed to replenish necessary food supplies, the seafaring families might be confined for generations in isolated enclaves, fostering the growth of distinctive languages, cultural mores, and physiological desires. It surely was a fundamental and difficult intellectual decision to abandon their familiar home for the unknown, but in successive waves, small family groups spread out to eventually cover the earth, as the sun, wind, and rain provided new places to live and the means to get there.

These people like us, of all shapes, sizes, and shades, possessed a unique talent unknown to earlier human beings—the ability to dream and wonder, to contemplate the future and remember the past, to be aware of the consequences of their actions. They discovered the pleasure of their skills and the desire to use them, to enjoy doing things better, and to be amazed that what they discovered was already there. Instead of gathering berries and hiding in caves, they learned how to plant and to hold food in clay cups. They invented agriculture and built a house to live in. When they discovered the ocean they invented the boat—maybe 8,000 years before the wheel. They had not invented radar, but their mind was constantly searching like one. They were definitely a new sort of human being that began to take nature apart and put it all together again.

To achieve the advanced lifestyle we live on Maui, we probably spent over 30,000 years in the process of exploration and experiment. In terms of the span of people like ourselves, the progressive patterns of human life have moved steadily through at least 16,000 generations, accelerating tremendously in the last 160—an incredibly brief span of history as we know it: the time required to take the first steps toward rational knowledge and the transit from the Stone Age, when they discovered, like a creative sculptor, that the many shapes in stone were always there.

It must have been an early discovery that monsoon winds in the Indian Ocean blew southerly in the winter and then reversed completely to blow toward the north in summer months. This knowledge and the discovery of the monsoon currents made it possible to sail in both directions along the African coast, and the discoverers ventured further and further from home. They did not need complicated sailing rigs—the wind was always behind them. With this knowledge, people could not resist sailing on. "Why did man do this?" asked Captain Alan Villiers. "He is a mobile creature. He has always had to move from place to place to seek food, flee invaders, to find new land, to trade—or simply to wander, to see what lies so tantalizingly over the horizon. Rivers offered paths through jungles, mountains, wastelands; seas linked islands. Man had to sail."

These were not migrations of people; probably at first only a few families looking for another place to farm, or an independent group dissatisfied with living in an organized community. It was the more venturesome explorers who first sailed ahead of monsoon winds into the Arbian Sea to the shores of the Persian Gulf, then a valley still to be drowned by the rising sea of melting ice. The rivers of glacial melt in a land of temperate climate and fertility, provided an ideal place to settle. In time the scattered families began gathering into larger communities for protection, and by about 8,500 B.C., people were living in what may have been the first small city, Jericho. Farmers and herders gradually moved overland from their first places of settlement into the fertile valley formed by silt from the Tigris and Euphrates rivers, as tribal groups calling themselves Elamites also sought shelter and agricultural opportunities in the marshes. Joining together, the people created new cities; became known as Sumerians, and by 3,500 B.C. had established the world's first civilization—Mesopotamia. Within another 1000 years, Egyptian civilization appeared in the lower Nile, a society formed by the descendants of those venturing into the Red Sea. About 2,500 B.C., seafarers who bypassed Persia to sail on toward India, had established the Indus civilization, centered in the Indus River delta and extending from Baluchistan to southern India.

Fabrication of copper, gold, and silver objects, and the production of bronze alloy, originated in the valleys of the Nile, Euphrates, and Indus, yet none of these burgeoning citystates possessed its own gold, silver, or copper ore. The need to import these increasingly needed metals parallel social and cultural interchange between the three civilizations on the rim of the Indian Ocean, spawning the beginnings of international ocean commerce between the ancient copper and silver mines in Oman at the mouth of the Persian Gulf and extensive ore deposits in Zimbabwe, central Africa. The Sumerians recorded trade with a land they called Makkan, their ocean-going ships importing gold, ivory, wood, semiprecious stones, and beads in exchange for Mesopotamian garments, wool, oil, and leather. When direct contact with Makkan was broken, the Sumerians used Bahrein as a point of exchange. The early records do not say where Makkan was.

An island in the Pacific; a small spot on the horizon; difficult to find unless you know it is there—symbolic of the island destination familiar to a thousand years of seafaring families. This is Ulul island, north of the equator and halfway across the Pacific Ocean—2,500 miles from Singapore and 2,900 miles from Maui. The ocean is so large, the distances so vast, the islands so small; that the first vague glimpse of shallow, green lagoon waters reflected in overhead clouds is carefully watched for, lest it vanish in the blink of an eye. There is comfort in these distant outlines of coconut palms and the imagined land at their base. Leaving the island for another destination, the island navigators do not finally commit themselves to the sea until the last glimpse of the last fronded silhouette.

Operators of trading vessels in the Indian Ocean invented the lateen sail rig, enabling their boats to maintain a course into the wind and not be so dependent on monsoon weather. Ship carpenters had long since developed construction methods for an efficient cargo-carrying vessel, the Arabian dhow, a slender-planked ship sewn together with fiber rope and then caulked. The trader captains gradually became capable of traveling almost anywhere, and migrating families continued eastward to settle new lands, even while others remained behind to populate cities, create civilizations, and wage war. The seafarers traveled along strange coasts, past southern India, across the Bay of Bengal, and southeast to what is now the Malay peninsula and Sumatra.

The same long, high prows on oceangoing Egyptian vessels, depicted on Nile temples, can be found on canoes seen on the Brahmaputra in Bangladesh. Bronze objects made in the Indus Valley and in Egypt have been found in Mesopotamia. The ocean trade between Africa and the three early civilizations is ample testimony to the ability of early seafarers in the Indian Ocean to repeatedly sail on long voyages to distant destinations, their navigational and sailing skills far surpassing those of contemporary Europe and Asia. Not until the Phoenicians carried their seafaring skills from the Persian Gulf into the Mediterranean would the peoples of Europe take interest in traveling on the ocean.

Phoenician sailors circumnavigated around Africa about 600 B.C., a feat not duplicated for 2,000 years. Herodotus explained, "When autumn came, they went ashore, wherever they might happen to be, and having sown a track of land with corn, waited until the grain was fit to cut. Having reaped it, they again set sail." The Phoenicians prepared a guide to coastal trading routes in the Indian Ocean, describing the seaports, how to get there, and politics of cities controlling trade and commerce. Possibly, it was the first travel book.

Those who sailed onward thousands of years before, across the northern Indian Ocean into Indonesian seas, settled onto exposed continental-shelf lands. There were few islands in southeast Asia before the end of the Ice Age—an almost continuous landmass extended from Thailand to Tasmania, south of Australia, broken only by narrow open passages in the Celebes Sea. The vast land area supporting a tropical jungle that few of the new arrivals ventured into.

Wild animals roamed the vast southeast wilderness. Elephant, orangutan, rhinoceros and tiger dominated forest life, and other predators and herbivores roamed unhindered from Thailand to Borneo. A thin strip of water prevented wildlife from venturing

Nan Madol, a 2,000 year old Venice in the Pacific, with fortress-temples constructed of basaltic lava on city-like blocks accessible by canals excavated from the coral reef. The walled city on Ponape Island once covered nine square miles and had more than 100 buildings.

eastward toward New Guinea; but it presented little difficulty to restless settlers who constructed canoes and sailed across onto the shelf land north of Australia to populate the subcontinent. In the next several hundred years still others explored the length of New Guinea and upon reaching the Coral Sea, resumed their travels in large double-hulled canoes, sailing eastward again to the Fiji islands and beyond. A small group traveled northward and the Philippines and China were settled. The fourth early civilization appeared in the Hwang Ho Valley of China, established on loess lands left behind by retreating glaciers. People from the China coast had already moved on into Siberia and across the Bering Strait to settle North and South America.

About the same time other groups on the eastern edge of southeast Asia launched canoes from their villages and sailed into the Pacific, resuming eastward migrations begun 10,000 years earlier in another ocean. Settlers traveling from the southern Philippines landed in Palau, and after several generations sailed east to Yap in Micronesia, gradually populating islands to the north in the Marianas. Another group, possibly sailing from northern Borneo into the Sulu Sea, found few islands in their path, until, turning northward, they discovered Kusaie and then Ponape Island in central Micronesia. Again repeating the traditional practices of their forebears over many generations, several families continued sailing eastward along the equator until they encountered a splay of islands scattered from the Marshalls in the north to Samoa in the south. Others stayed behind on the island they discovered and built a city.

On Ponape Island in the remote central Pacific, the oceanic pioneers created an astonishing city designed on a grid of Venetian-style canals in which Othello would have felt at home—a city of canal streets dredged from the fringing coral reef. The builders, still carrying with them after thousands of ocean miles the inventive skills of craftsmen long dead, erected stone fortress-temples of basaltic, columnar volcanic rock hauled from distant quarries. Some rocks weighed five tons.

This Venice in the Pacific was conceived by two brothers, Olsihpa and Olsohpa. They called the city Nan Madol (Place of the Spaces), a Pacific island city that survived for 2,000 years before succumbing to tropical storms and disease brought into the islands by European explorers. The island builders were descendants of voyagers who first ventured into the Pacific a thousand years earlier; but the layout plan of Nan Madol's temples, perhaps not unexpectedly, was not new, but closely conformed to the design of stone temples in southern India. The rafts used to transport heavy lava blocks to construction sites could not have been unlike the Nile transporters devised by Egyptians. Their outrigger canoes were of the same basic design as canoes still in use by Andaman islanders in the Bay of Bengal. The Pacific islanders needed no written language to transmit these skills over a hundred generations.

In the first century after abandonment, typhoons broke down aging stone dikes and silted in the canals. Waves swept inland, undermining temple foundations. Breadfruit trees and coconut palms split canal revetments, and mangrove thickets flourished in the sandy canals. Vines were trailing from temple walls and Nan Madol was entirely overgrown by jungle when German colonial administrators heard of a "phantom city" on the reef. Ponapeans warned German archaeologists to not disturb the bones of buried royalty, but the German governor persisted in digging personally in the old tombs. One night the governor was kept awake by odd sounds from Nan Madol. The next day he was dead. The curse of the Ponapean Nahnmwarkis is as potent as that of the pharaohs.

The Samoan and Tongan islands were settled while Nan Madol was built and small exploratory groups continued eastward, as if an irresistible force urged the seafarers to forever seek new lands and living space. They gained considerable knowledge of the movement of stars in the Southern Hemisphere, and soon were capable of determining their position and course beyond the sight of familiar landmarks with relative ease. As navigators learned the behavior of shifting ocean currents and seasonal changes in wind patterns, their ability to complete return voyages accelerated social interchange between the hundreds of South Pacific islands, and the genesis of an oceanic nation manifested itself in the centuries before Europeans ventured into the Pacific ocean islands.

Like people today, some were content to stay behind and grow only the food they needed; to build a country home for themselves and stay out of the city. Others were restless and moved on, to build civilizations. Those islanders who did not want powered boats and tin roofs sit back and watch from their grass-thatched huts in rare good humor, possibly wiser and healthier than all the others; eating yams from their own gardens, and enjoying the sun with no imported clothes. For after the minerals and oil are all gone, those who stayed behind and refused to participate in building civilizations, refused to dig and drill and saw, respecting the land and living on it, not by it, may still enjoy a way of life inherited from their ancestors who started it all so many thousands of years ago.

Design details of Micronesian outrigger canoes, here photographed in the remote central Pacific Namonuito Atoll, are identical on all islands of the same cultural group, yet no construction drawings exist—the necessary design information is passed on from family to family as part of an oral inheritance.

The capability of outrigger canoes is proven in the efficient designs still in use. Sailing on the open ocean in craft designed a thousand years ago is a unique thrill obtainable in remote island archipelagos. The ability to navigate by the stars without compass or sextant is a skill still in use on Pacific ocean waters.

The others continued on—still looking. After Samoa they discovered Tahiti and began populating surrounding islands. Sailing eastward apparently continued to intrigue the chiefs of Tahiti, and the older, more experienced navigators talked of exploring beyond the Marquesas. It was probably thought of as a routine voyage of a few weeks' duration before returning to compare observations; or perhaps several enthusiastic fishermen chasing a school of yellow-fin tuna found themselves unable to return against unfavorable winds and searched for a refuge. They found Easter Island.

"Far to the southeast of the Marquesas lies evidence of a truly remarkable feat," wrote Bishop Museum anthropologist Kenneth Emory. "A voyage to Easter Island, some 2,400 miles away, in the face of prevailing winds and currents. Polynesia's easternmost outpost, Easter Island is not only the most isolated inhabited island in the Pacific, but it is also only fifteen miles long."

About A.D. 750 another remarkable voyage occurred, testimony to the overwhelming skill of Polynesian navigators. Leaving Tahiti on one of the few deliberate westward voyages, a cluster of double-hulled canoes loaded heavily with provisions for a long sea crossing, including family groups to establish new communities on distant islands, sailed for many weeks to a landfall, New Zealand, 2,500 miles southwest. Those who settled there called themselves Maoris. Like the settlers who sailed southwest across the Indian Ocean to find Madagascar almost 2,000 years earlier, these people, also, never made a return voyage to their home islands.

Fishing far northeast of the Marquesas where they had never ventured before, another group of adventurous sailors found themselves in the doldrums, a belt of calm and light variable winds just north of the equator. Drifting northward they were caught in the westerly trades and blown steadily in the direction of unknown islands, first observed a hundred or so miles away, from the glow of erupting volcanoes reflected in high clouds overhead. It was the Hawaiian archipelago, another discovery for the Polynesians. Return voyages were made and the largest Hawaiian island, immediately south of Maui, became an outpost of the Marquesan ruling oligarchy.

During this most spectacular and concluding era of Polynesian exploration, after Easter Island was discovered and about the same time the Maoris sailed southwest, the king of Tahiti sent important chiefs and families on an extended northern voyage of discovery. Aware that there probably were more islands north of Tahiti, he intended to find them, and his fleet of canoes encountered the first a week's sail away, Christmas Island. A few days' sail further on they came upon Fanning Island, where a small rock shrine was dedicated to protective gods. Continuing northward they finally made landfall on Necker Island, beyond Kaua'i. On rocky Necker, they constructed another shrine to invoke the gods before exploring the Hawaiian islands, looking for the best, the most suitable island living place. They eventually landed on the Maui shore below an erupting volcanic peak they named Haleakala (House of the Sun), on a point of land they called Kahikinui (Great Tahiti)—the last landfall on a 10,000-year voyage; on the last uninhabited land in the world to be settled.

The new settlers lived relatively gently upon the land. In the early decades after settlement there was ample food for the small population, and people respected the obvious limits of an island's resources. It is said that in these times, after a giant ko'a canoe log was cut in the high forest, the ground was prepared to encourage seedlings. And collectors of yellow and red feathers for the magnificent royal capes, snared birds only long enough to pluck individual feathers and let the birds fly free. At fish-spawning periods, taking fish was prohibited in areas marked by coconut fronds and during other months certain seaweeds were kapu, to help preserve inshore fisheries.

The weather was ideal, pesky flies and mosquitoes unknown, no snakes or poisonous spiders, and a generally free society with few restrictive encumbrances. The early Hawaii days might be compared to the sought-after Arcadian paradise, but it was not to be for long. Ambitious remnants of Tahitian royalty soon forbade the making of return trips to Tahiti, and began building their own Hawaii tribal oligarchy. The Hawaiians had started late, but it would not be long before they, too, put into effect some of the more annoying attributes of civilization.

As available lands became limited and agricultural valleys suitable for irrigation and taro growing were occupied, rival factions of ruling ali'i began dividing the islands into pie-shaped ahupua'a, extending from central mountaintops to the sea. Use of the ahupua'a were controlled by the ali'i, and commoners lived on the land at the pleasure of ali'i, paid taxes in food and products, and fought in the numerous island wars at their call. There evolved a well-ordered feudal lifestyle, part of a royal kapu system to assure control by the ali'i over their subjects and food resources. The ancient kapu system had been carried across the Pacific from southeast Asia and continuously modified enroute over many generations, with infusions based on changing oceanic attitudes.

The taro in Halawa Valley was planted by the first Polynesians settling on Maui and was harvested to make poi for over 300 years until a tsunami wave on April Fool's Day, 1946 wiped out the ancient patches. They were never replanted.

Kapu is associated with mana, a powerful supernatural and impersonal force, often embodied in inanimate objects and sometimes in human beings. To the ali'i was ascribed great mana, because the kahuna priest said he was descended from the gods. Under the kapu system enforced by kahunas, life was severely restricted: certain fish could not be eaten by women, and, where the ahupua'a did not reach the sea, people in that district could not fish along the shore. Fishponds were constructed to raise fish exclusively for the ali'i, and the kahuna made it very clear that the commoner owed the ali'i his life, and any violation of the kapu or failure in the performance of duties toward the ali'i would result in death.

The Hawaiian commoner had no individual liberty, owned no land, and was not allowed to even use a surfboard—surfing was reserved for the ali'i. The people could not bathe on certain reserved beaches; men could not eat with their women, and women could not eat certain foods reserved for the men. Violators of the kapu might be strangled or clubbed to death by ali'i, who controlled almost everything the commoner did. When the ali'i walked upon the coastal trail, retainers ran ahead to warn of his approach so his subjects would be prostrate upon his arrival.

The ethnocentric European historians have a way of defining their own tradition into predominance. "Polynesia produced no Dante, Michelangelo, Shakespeare, Newton or Goethe," writes Kenneth Clark. "The very fragility of those Arcadian societies," Clark continues, in reference to Pacific cultures, "the speed and completeness with which they collapsed on the peaceful appearance of a few British sailors followed by a handful of missionaries—shows that they were not civilizations . . ." The rise of southeast Asian and oceanic civilizations, nevertheless, was proceeding apace, from Angkor Wat in Cambodia and Nan Madol in Ponape, to Tahiti in the South Pacific, when their flowering was abruptly halted by European colonists. Perhaps not quite as violently as Spanish conquerors of native Indian cities in Mexico and South America, but just as completely.

The British, German, French, and Spanish sailors did use their guns on occasion to enforce exclusive trading rights and sovereignty, as European cartographers arbitrarily divided up the Pacific islands between themselves; but their task of subjugation was made easy by accompanying legions of microbes—spirochetae, gonococci, and viruses—and it was these tiny allies that accomplished the decline of incipient island civilizations. The Europeans were mucopurulent, unclean—a civilization that effected its superiority through venereal disease.

While Europeans were still rowing and afraid to venture too far into an unknown ocean, lest they fall off the edge, oceanic peoples were sailing oceans with fore-and-aft rigged sail and centerboard, relying on the same aerodynamic principle as modern aircraft. Their accomplishments in navigation and logistics and their daring to face the unknown in long voyages of exploration surpassed in certain respects those of Magellan and Cook thousands of years later. The European explorers returned home with copious notes, charts, and flower samples; oceanic peoples sailed with family groups, domestic animals, and seeds for new island civilizations. They needed no charts. British explorer James Cook wrote of their uncommon skills in his journal, "The sun serves as compass by day and the moon and stars by night."

These people who settled the Pacific were architects, politicians, and master navigators. They amassed an extraordinary knowledge of the ocean and sky and applied it expertly to maritime skills. Astronomical systems were devised not for the planting of crops, but to guide seagoing navigtors. Herman Friis, in his history of the Pacific basin, writes that "a far-flung network of inter-island exchange and refinement of knowledge bore fruit in the development of a rudimentary science, a definite international system . . . only the European impact interrupted a spreading process whereby sidereal and lunar months were being coordinated." Captain Cook, well aware of the adverse consequences of his presence in the Pacific, later referred to his visits as "the fatal impact." The introduction of alien cultures, animals and plants, begun by Cook and expeditions that followed, permanently upset the delicate ecological balance between the Hawaiian islanders and their fragile island environment.

When Cook sailed north from Tahiti on his last voyage of Pacific exploration, he must have known where he was going. The king of Tahiti, with whom he conferred before departure, undoubtedly informed him fully of the Hawaiian islands to the north, and convenient landfalls enroute, all excellent stops for fresh foods and water. His plotted course shows no erratic wandering around the ocean. Cook sailed direct to Christmas Island, so named because he arrived on the holiday, and located his intended Kaua'i landfall on schedule.

Stopping for only a few days on Kaua'i, he sailed to the Pacific northwest and into Bering Strait, searching unsuccessfully for a northwest passage back to England, before returning to Hawaii for the winter. Cooks' two vessels, the *Resolution* and *Discovery*, first dropped anchor off Maui's north shore at Wailua, the apparent floating temples with "sails like a stingray and caves in the sides with shining holes behind," causing considerable commotion among the Hawaiians.

Cook's ships arrived during a pause in Hawaii's recurring internecine warfare: the bloody battles between ali'i on every island, fought by warriors who sometimes celebrated victories by killing the families of defeated forces. Kalani'opu'u and a young

Kamehameha had invaded Maui in a fleet of canoes from the Big Island and were then fighting in Hana. Kamehameha would later conquer all the islands to establish the Kingdom of Hawaii, but in the Hana battles he was learning the skills of warfare. In Hamoa he saved the life of his instructor, whose feet became entangled in sweet potato vines. While the tutor struggled to free himself, Kamehameha held off attacking Mauians by grabbing the naked warriors between the legs and jerking them off their feet. Kamehameha went on to conquer all the islands except Kaua'i, and became first king of Hawaii.

Knowledge of the incessant fighting encouraged the church to send missionaries to Hawaii; but before their arrival the Hawaiians themselves banished the cruel kapu system, rejected the kahuna priests, and began destroying temple images. A religious vacuum existed and the fundamentalist reverends from America wasted no time in teaching their own version of what a community should believe in, quickly creating a written Hawaiian language to spread the word of their Christian God, introducing to the islanders a New England style of living, and covering the "naked, heathen bodies" of the Hawaiian "savages."

The arrival of the missionary, despite the church's rigid ways, soon meant emancipation for ordinary Hawaiians, who had no rights in their feudal community. It must be said that Hawaii commoners were treated far worse by their contemporaries than by the haole who eventually took over their islands. The pioneering traders, sugar planters, and cattle ranchers were to eventually introduce a capitalistic democracy, quite limited in its application and often racist, but nevertheless a considerable improvement over the cruel and corrupt methods of Hawaiian ali'i.

On busy Front Street in Lahaina, almost hidden under shade trees that soften the noise of tourist traffic, sits a restored two-story house looking as if it had been carefully lifted from a New England seaport town and transferred intact to this old historic whaling port. Henry Perrine Baldwin, one of the original partners of Alexander & Baldwin, was born here on August 29, 1842. He was one of the sugar planters who helped transform the islands from a kingdom into a republic.

His father was the missionary doctor Dwight Baldwin, who arrived in Lahaina in 1835 after serving four years as a doctor at the church rest station in Waimea on the Big Island. Rev. Baldwin welcomed the assignment to Lahaina, thinking he would be able to devote himself fully to mssionary work, but soon learned that he was the only missionary on Maui, Moloka'i, or Lana'i qualified to practice medicine.

Baldwin's home was built by his predecessor in 1834 of hand-hewn timbers, with thick walls of coral and stone. He added a bedroom and study in 1840, and nine years later a second story to house the family's six new children. He set his dining room table with Blue Willow china, and received patients in the study, where he administered to sick and dying Hawaiians during the smallpox epidemic of 1853. At night whale oil was used to light the lamps, and a barrel of oil donated by a friendly sea captain would last a year. Flour was brought around the Horn, sometimes becoming so wet by the time it was delivered in Lahaina that Mrs. Baldwin had to chisel off the daily measure for cooking. The family's mainland vegetable garden was out back, and island breadfruit, bananas, and mangoes were was available for picking.

Henry Baldwin grew up in the missionary home, sharing with his brother, Charles, a large bedroom on the second floor. Another room in the north wing was used as a combination dispensary and school, where his father and mother were the only teachers. Both brothers learned to swim like natives in the Lahaina surf, taught by their Hawaii nurse, Kealoha and the young boy developed an aptitude for music and led morning hymns and evening prayer on the melodeon, playing for services at the nearby Seaman's Chapel where his father preached.

The comfortable home was visited often by missionary families, government officials, and captains of whaling ships. In 1843 the William P. Alexander family arrived to take over Lahainaluna School, in the hills above Lahaina. With the new family was their son, Samuel T. Alexander, the boy who was destined to become Henry Baldwin's business partner. He was seven at the time.

Sugarcane was not the only crop raised for export on Maui. No other agricultural activity, except pineapple, approached the success of sugar, but at different times, cotton, mulberry trees for silk, rubber trees, sisal for manila hemp, and arrowroot were grown on island farms. Both foreigners and natives planted fruits and vegetables for overseas markets. Irish potatoes and yams grew so well in Kula that a steady stream of horse-drawn wagons carried barrels of potatoes to sailing schooners waiting at Kahului Harbor.

When gold was discovered in California, Maui's farmers were ready for the boom. In 1850, Kula was called Nu Kaleponi (New California), because the fertile soil, capable of growing crops the year around, yielded as much wealth to Hawaiians as California gold mines to mainlanders. Ships docked in increasing numbers to get cargoes of fresh produce to supply the hordes of miners sweeping into the Sierra Nevada foothills, some carrying children of wealthy San Franciscans sending their offspring to Lahainaluna for schooling in the best private school west of the Mississippi. Wild sugar brought in from Hana found a ready market among Chinese laborers working California mines, and native families not only neglected their taro patches, but also the missionaries' call to prayer, as they became farmers in a new kind of economic world, growing strange new foods for people they never saw.

Samuel T. Alexander   Henry P. Baldwin

Henry Baldwin courted and married Sam Alexander's sister, Emily, after the new partners bought their first piece of land in 1869, a Hawaiian kuleana of nearly twelve acres, for $110. Within eight years from that first purchase the Alexander and Baldwin plantation was planting 2,000 acres of land, possessed a large mortgage, an inefficient mill, and the growing knowledge that all would be lost if their arid land in central Maui was not irrigated.

Working in the mill one afternoon with his engineer, Baldwin was studying the adjustment on the roller train that crushed the cane when, in an effort to demonstrate that the gap between the rollers was larger on one side than the other, he slipped his right hand into the opening. Before the machine could be stopped, Baldwin's arm was crushed to the elbow. He drank a stiff tot of brandy while cooly instructing a messenger to ride quickly and fetch his doctor in Wailuku, ten miles away. "Ride swiftly to the doctor's," said Baldwin, "but for the horse's sake, return at a walk."

The doctor saw a rider in the distance, racing across the flat plains to his house and prepared for the worst, collected his medical bag, saddled his horse, and met the rider at the gate. The messenger returned with the doctor at full clip and his horse died shortly thereafter, a loss which Baldwin apparently regretted almost as much as the arm he lost that afternoon. Two weeks later Baldwin was writing letters with his left hand and had ordered two new organs, one for his home and the other for a church at Makawao where he was now organist. Both could be played with one hand while he did the bass parts with his feet.

The same year, Alexander and Baldwin obtained a lease from the kingdom to construct a seventeen-mile aqueduct on crown lands to bring irrigation water to their sugar fields in central Maui. Alexander's younger brother did the survey, and he prepared plans for a ditch to intercept and collect water from streams between Honopou and Naili'iliha'ele valleys in East Maui. The government agreement required the partners to complete construction within two years or the ditch would revert to the kingdom. Alexander estimated the project would be completed in months and cost about $50,000. The necessary money was raised to get started and Baldwin took over from there to see the Hamakua Ditch through to completion.

Alexander and Baldwin enjoyed a good working relationship; it played an important part in making the controversial ditch project a success. Doubters, convinced such a ditch could not be built, were many, and the pair could not have anticipated the events that brought the project to the brink of failure. Alexander was the idea man; Baldwin, the doer. These complementary natures solved a variety of difficult problems and made their joint venture fruitful.

Although Baldwin lost his right arm only months before the digging started, he wasted no time in putting together a crew, which at times numbered 200, and began work. There wasn't a trained engineer in the lot. The superintendent was a carpenter, overseers were shipwrecked sailors from Lahaina, and the rest were general laborers with no experience in constructing an aqueduct. Most of the work was routine up to the east side of Maliko Gulch, a ravine 300 feet deep and 800 feet wide. It was July 6, 1877, when they reached the gulch and they had over a year, according to their lease, to get to the other side.

Downhill from Maliko and across the dry fields along the shore at lower Pa'ia are the remnants of an old plantation camp, Spreckelsville. Certainly it gives no hint today of the history made here a hundred years ago. The haole name is from Claus Spreckels, a California financier and sugar refiner, who sailed to Maui on his second visit to the islands in 1877, intending to transform the fledgling Hawaii sugar industry into a profitable enterprise for himself. The United States had signed the Reciprocity Treaty with King David Kalakaua, which provided duty-free admission of sugar and other products into the United States. Hawaii sugar planters received almost the entire benefit of the tariff remission, about two cents a pound, and Spreckels decided it was time he became a Hawaii sugar planter.

Not much aloha was extended Spreckels, who was looked upon as somewhat of an interloper on Maui, an outsider to kama'aina, island-born families who considered Hawaii their exclusive economic domain. But Spreckels quickly became a close friend and constant gambling companion of King Kalakaua. It was during one of their marathon poker games that King Kalakaua reputedly displayed his winning hand, saying, "I have five kings," pointing to himself as the fifth.

Presenting a contradictory image to his admirers, King Kalakaua appeared to decry the increasing influence of foreign businessmen in Hawaii at the same time he was helping them acquire more land. Hawaiian cultural traditions in dance and music, which missionaries had long banned as corrupt and indecent, were brought out of hidden closets, encouraged by the king to again be part of Hawaii life. The Royal Hawaiian Band played again and sensuous hulas were revived. Chants and ancient hula mele were recorded for posterity. Yet, while evoking a renaissance of old Hawaii, he conspired with others to corrupt the throne, on one occasion accepting payments from two separate individuals for exclusive rights to sell opium in Hawaii. He was called the "Merrie Monarch," a man of letters, and a cultural intermediary between a changing Hawaii he could not understand and the ancient Hawaiian ways he evidently yearned for. He was Hawaii's last king, and possibly his own worst enemy.

Spreckels developed a plan of his own for a longer, thirty-mile, irrigation ditch to water cane land he had acquired near Kahului, and asked Kalakaua for water rights in the same watershed as Alexander and Baldwin. In a midnight order, the king dismissed his less than supportive cabinet, appointed new members sympathetic to Spreckels' petition, and water rights were granted Spreckels in a signed order the following week. The lease stipulated that if Alexander and Baldwin's Hamakua Ditch was not completed within their two-year working period, as previously agreed, then Spreckels would not only receive a license for a second ditch but would take over Hamakua Ditch as well. The king's cashbook shows a loan of $4,000 from Claus Spreckels dated the same day his lease was signed.

Suddenly, the deadline to finish Hamakua Ditch was a more serious matter. Alexander had already worried about crossing Maliko Gulch, and predicted that the problems to be encountered would be the "most formidable we will have to contend with." His plan was to pipe water across the gulch by means of a 1,100-foot-long eighteen-inch inverted iron syphon. It would be necessary for workers to lower themselves down the precipitous gulch walls by rope, hand over hand above the threatening rocks hundreds of feet below. The workers at first refused. Baldwin decided he must make the first leap and give the laborers courage. Clutching the rope with his legs and one arm, he swung 300 feet into the gulch, urging the workers to follow. Baldwin repeated the feat every day until the syphon was completed down into the gulch and up the opposite side. The deadline was met, and the ditch was theirs. It cost $80,000 to build, more than Alexander had budgeted, but the ditch served more than one purpose. Not only did it allow sugarcane to be cultivated profitably on the dry, sandy fields in central Maui, but the ditch became a model for other irrigation projects throughout the kingdom.

Spreckels stubbornly went on to build his own parallel ditch that would eventually be combined with Hamakua Ditch to become the largest privately built irrigation system in the United States—a ditch system unique in the world. Maui was well on its way to becoming a very different living place. Neither the Hawaiians nor the missionaries had in mind what Spreckels, Alexander, and Baldwin were doing in the islands.

Engineers brought to Maui by Spreckels constructed one of the most efficient sugar mills in the world, inventing a twenty-four-hour process for refining sugar that saved considerable time and money, compared with the old two-week method. In 1881 the first electric lights lit his sugar mill, located in the town he unblushingly called Spreckelsville, five years before royalty's Iolani Palace in Honolulu was wired for electricity. The Kahului Railroad ran an "Ali'i Special," carrying Kalakaua Dowager Queen Emma and Princess Ruth Ke'ilikolani to view the mill grinding cane at night—a sight never before seen in the world.

At Spreckelsville the first railroads were introduced to haul harvested cane from the fields, the first steam plow was used, and the first five-roller mill installed. His company, Hawaiian Commercial & Sugar, became by 1882 the most modern and largest sugar company in the world. The cane was grown on about 25,000 acres in central Maui that he acquired through devices ranging from routine business transactions, connivance with scheming Hawaiians, to outright blackmail of the Hawaiian kingdom. Over the next ten years Spreckels continued to expand his industrial monopoly, and to the consternation of Henry Baldwin, Spreckels was buying everybody else's raw sugar and attempting to acquire all or most of every company that touched Hawaiian sugar. The steamship company that carried sugar across the Pacific to San Francisco was his, raw sugar was refined at a Spreckels-owned refinery on the coast, and the profits deposited in his own bank.

All this must have influenced his friend Kalakaua, who had started to think of himself as more than just an island king and had begun to emulate the sovereigns of Europe. Kalakaua thought he would like to be king of Oceania, or at least of Polynesia, and purchased an aged steamer in need of overhaul, signed on a crew of reform school students, and installed loaded cannon on the front deck. The king sent his ambassador plenipotentiary to Samoa for his first conquest. He had considered the Marshall Islands, but the British were already there. When his "navy" arrived in Samoa, the Germans, who were having some of their own colonial problems, directed that Kalakaua's representative should leave Samoa on the next tide. His imperial ambitions were never heard of again, but he did achieve another distinction: Kalakaua, on a voyage to England to pay his respects to Queen Victoria, became the first royal sovereign to circumnavigate the globe.

In 1886, disagreement over competitive services arose between Spreckels and the owners of Kahului Railroad, and Spreckels struck back in characteristic style. He owned a five-acre plot of land across the railroad's right-of-way to harbor piers, and halted all railroad operations over his land. He refused to sell. When KRR initiated legal action, Spreckels retaliated by organizing another railroad and steamship firm, registering it as a public utility, and transferring HC&S land ringing Kahului Harbor over to the new com-

About 1925, a Kahului Railroad locomotive pulls a mixed freight to
Ha'iku across the Maliko Gulch steel railroad trestle. Built around 1909,
the trestle structure also carried the new steel pipeline for Ha'iku Ditch
water from the wet side of the island.

pany, continuing to block all access to the harbor. Samuel Alexander was outraged, and
organized a syndicate of independent Maui plantations not yet caught in the Spreckels
net to directly challenge the monopoly. Henry Baldwin joined Alexander, and the partners who already owned a minority interest in HC&S, purchased the majority stock in
HC&S along with KRR, its rolling stock and merchandise, to gain control of both the
railroad and port facilities.

Spreckels continued to control his new railroad and steamship company, and in a final
sputter of perniciousness, shut off both HC&S and KRR from the port. Finally, in 1899,
when the new owners of HC&S acquired Spreckels' embryonic utility, the two railroads
merged into one and a new Maui financial team, Alexander & Baldwin, gained control
of Kahului Harbor.

By 1898, aloha for Spreckels was running thin. After finding a disagreeable drawing
and a threatening note nailed to the front gate of his Honolulu home, Spreckels decided
to leave, sailing at noon the next day. Newspapers of the time reported his household
staff had not made the beds or washed breakfast dishes before his hasty departure. At
the dock he swore, ''I'll not return 'till grass grows on Fort Street.'' He never did.

Financing harbor improvements with private funds, A&B developed Kahului into a
modern shipping facility, and began diversifying its corporate holdings to include mer-
chandising, insurance, railroads, land development, and a shipping company to carry its

sugar to West Coast ports. A&B first invested in Matson Navigation Company in 1909, along with other Hawaii sugar companies, and Matson soon became the leading carrier of passengers and cargo between the West Coast and Hawaii. Matson's famous passenger liner *Lurline* carried thousands of tourists on their first Hawaii visit, and the Royal Hawaiian Hotel was built by Matson in 1927 to accommodate the increasing numbers of visitors arriving to enjoy Waikiki Beach. It was the beginning of Hawaii's tourist industry. A&B began packing pineapple and organized 'Ulupalakua Ranch on the southwest slope of Haleakala. At one time A&B, through Matson, even became part owner of an oil pipeline company.

During World War II, Matson ships sailed on all the oceans, and Matson repaired and maintained trans-Pacific transport aircraft for the navy in California, and made plans to begin air service to Hawaii after the war. The first flight was completed in a DC-4, the *Sky Matsonia*; but the CAB denied Matson's application for scheduled air passenger service, asserting that appropriate competition would not occur when the airline was owned by a steamship company plying the same route.

Alexander and Baldwin, as investing partners, owned part of Inter-Island Steam Navigation Company, which started Inter-Island Airways and became Hawaiian Air. The airline developed, on its own, the original inter-island air navigation system, and airline Captain James Hogg set up instrument landing letdown procedures for all the islands. After the airline constructed its own direction-finding station at Kahului, then called MAU, federal aviation officials decided they should give credit where due and proposed designating the facility after Captain Hogg. They asked whether he wanted the first three letters of his name or the last three. He chose the last three, so today the international airline code for Maui is not HOG, but OGG.

In 1964, the United States Justice Department decided that the ownership of Matson by A&B and all the other major sugar producers in Hawaii (the "Big Five" as it was called), all major customers of Matson, constituted an anti-trust violation. So A&B, in a simple solution to the problem, bought out most of the other part-owners to acquire controlling interest in the company. By 1969 A&B owned all of Matson and encouraged the development of the first integrated ocean freight research department, leading to Matson's invention of the containership that revolutionized ocean cargo shipping. What began on Maui was now beginning to affect the world.

The Alexanders and Baldwins and other Hawaii planters were never able to convince native Hawaiians to work for them in the sugar and pineapple fields. It was too easy to go fishing, to grow your own food, and to build your own thatched hut. Along with others in Hawaii's sugar industry, the decision was made to import contract labor from overseas. First came the Chinese workers, then the Japanese. Workers from Scotland were hired and, in 1881, Norwegians and Germans arrived, followed by Gilbert Islanders and Portuguese. Filipinos were the last laborers to be imported after the war, to join with the others in a new home, following the early Hawaiians and pioneering Americans to the islands of Hawaii.

In the years following World War II, increasing numbers of tourists returned to stay—finding Hawaii a better place to live. Statehood brought in millions of investment dollars and when scheduled jets began flying—moving Hawaii to an easy four hours from California—tourism began growing at rates approaching twenty percent a year. Then Maui was discovered by the Canadians and Maui developers began building condominiums at about the same rate. After a national poll identified Hawaii as the "most desired vacation," the only problem was where to put all the hotels. Then local residents and environmentalists began to ask, "How many tourists are too many?"

When Matson became part of A&B, 1,450 acres of Matson-owned kiawe forest and sand dunes along the Wailea shore had been designated by the state planning office as a "tourist destination area" on the first State General Plan prepared in the nation. In partnership with the Northwestern Mutual Life Insurance Company, A&B soon became a Maui resort developer on lands that Matson had acquired from 'Ulupalakua Ranch, then owned by Frank Baldwin, son of Henry Baldwin from Lahaina.

The Hawaiians arrived first, followed by the missionairies, whose children often metamorphosed into skilled businessmen. Then came the whalers and traders. Now it is the turn of still more people from around the world to continue what the Hawaii people began on their long ocean voyages: the newest immigrants with their ideas and mainland traditions from north and south, blending easily into the island lifestyle already rich in Far East and Pacific cultures. Hawaii and Maui accept it all as people continue to arrive—tourists and residents to be—bringing to Maui the excitement of new ways to live on the best of islands: the last place to settle on earth. □

The young people of Maui are the inheritors of a rich cultural diversity that continues to mature, enhancing their own living place and the island home of newer immigrants still arriving.

An unnamed waterfall in the Kipahulu Valley section of Haleakala National Park is within one of two national park working cattle ranches in the nation. It is part of a new national park land use philosophy to preserve cultural lifestyles and pastoral beauty as well as traditional natural scenic resources. A portion of the lands planned for inclusion in the park may be set aside for Hawaii people to use in traditional ways, such as rural subsistence living now rapidly disappearing.

The Nene, an endangered native Hawaii goose, was reduced to about three dozen pairs before bird fanciers in Hawaii and England succeeded in keeping newly hatched birds alive, saving the Nene from extinction. After banded birds were released in Haleakala Crater, a pair from England and Hawaii were observed on Mauna Kea. Apparently a local bird from Hawaii Island, released on Maui, had mated with an immigrant bird from England, and together they flew to a new home across the channel on Hawaii Island.

Lahaina . . . the image of the South Pacific captured in the colors of Gauguin and the words of Nordhoff and Hall . . . an American version of French Papeete as crowded and noisy as the original. The restored sailing ship *Carthaginian*, a reminder of Lahaina's whaling heritage, is moored in front of the century-old Pioneer Inn, oldest hotel in Hawaii and still open to visitors from far-distant ports. Sweeping above Lahaina town, fields of sugarcane merge into the mountains and valleys of Maui.

A geologic drama of long ago created and molded these oceanic islands into unique shapes and textures. Breaking surf defines the peninsula of Keʻanae, an ancient lava flow from Haleakala's Koʻolau Gap, into a stark black, white, and blue meeting of the land and sea. Taro patches (overleaf) are geometric patterns in irrigated fields that have produced poi for generations. ⟿

The story was first told many years ago. When the builders of St. Gabriel's mission in Wailua needed coral blocks and sand to finish construction; waves from a provident storm heaped the needed materials upon a nearby shore in a single night. Residents are still grateful, and the shoulders of the life-sized Christ at St. Gabriel's are often draped with a lei of flowers.

The mountain slopes west of Haleakala below the national park boundary lines are seldom seen by visitors except as a hazy outline during the morning hours before tradewind clouds move into higher elevations. The temperate zone climate on the mountain is a delightful break from the tropics below, with occasional snow in the winter and fog and rain nearly every afternoon. On the mile high pastures of 'Ulupalakua Ranch continuous green covers the landscape. Above the ranch, forests of redwood, cedar, and fir convert the ridgeline into a landscape reminiscent of Washington State. At Polipoli Springs, the view through evergreen firs to the West Maui Mountains is, indeed, a view like another world.

Makena and Wailea are side by side geographically, but a vast distance separates them on the cultural and economic scale. At the Hotel Inter-Continental Maui pool, emphasis is on luxury by the sea, while at Makena Beach the lifestyle of a simpler and earlier time continues to prevail. Where the smooth and newly paved road abruptly ends and the rough cinder-graded road begins, a visitor intrudes upon an environment little touched by imported accouterments of resort life. Where dogs play today on the beach is where island people still live by the beach. Puʻu ʻOʻili and Kahoʻolawe Island outline the horizon.

Makena. The last wild part of Maui's west shore, with isolated beaches, kiawe thickets, and tumbled rocks of ancient Hawaii villages, is a controversial issue between resort developers and environmentalists. A drive through Makena to the end of the rough cinder road at La Perouse is a visit to old Hawaii, where people still live by the sea and from the sea. Perhaps if the west shore beyond Wailea should remain forever wild, it would be in the best interests of all Maui.

2

The Years on *Our* Land—An Island in the Sun

I took a quick glance inside our small cabin on the second deck, reserved for the over-night voyage from Honolulu to Kahului, and decided it would be wiser to stay up all night and keep walking around outside. The Moloka'i Channel waves were typical of every winter, characteristically doubling up on each other with windblown chops trying to climb on the back of sets generated by seasonal crosscurrents. A twenty-foot swell, measured from trough to crest, was not uncommon.

On occasion the bow dipped in the black water ahead and tossed parts of a wave from bow to stern, like tossing a shawl over its shoulder. Hanging tightly to the top deck rail-ing with a small group of passengers grimly facing into each wave as if it were a personal challenge, I marveled at the ability of our ship, the cattle boat *Humu'ula,* to stay afloat in the storm, and at my ability to keep down the contents of my increasingly queasy stomach. The routine slap in the face from cold water sweeping over the deckhouse must receive full credit. My bride and I were sailing for Hana on our honeymoon. It was 1944, during the war years, and inter-island steamers were the scenic way to travel in Hawaii, as the windows of DC-3 passenger aircraft were blacked out. Flying between the islands was like buying a ticket in a submarine, and I'd still get airsick.

The only public ground transportation to Hana during the war years was Redo's bread truck, and we introduced ourselves to the driver parked outside Kashiwa's Bakery in Kahului, while he finished loading large red boxes of fresh bread intended for delivery at every store from Pa'ia to Hana. Piled high in the stake-body truck were crates of live chickens, a couple of pigs, two-fifty gallon barrels of kerosene and bags of potatoes, onions, and lettuce for Hasegawa General Store. The driver told us to sit on top of it all and we climbed aboard, choosing a bag of onions as perhaps the softest freight to sit on. We shifted around, trying in turn every bag, box, and barrel, arriving in Hana at the end of a long day standing up in the rocking truck.

Redo stopped everywhere along the rough unpaved Hana Road—at Kailua, Ke'anae, Wailua, Nahiku, and several unnamed stops in the middle of nowhere—to greet a customer or friend. The trip was a grand introduction to rural Maui and a lifestyle that still thrives today, thanks to the narrow, many curved highway that fortunately has proven too expensive to improve. Hana people like it the way it is, enjoy their isolation, and talk of establishing a ''pothole maintenance committee'' to discourage too many visitors driving on their road. They have no desire to welcome the rest of the world.

On this first trip to Hana, no hotel existed. We stayed upstairs over Okada General Store, across the road from Hasegawa General Store, in rooms originally rented to single Japanese men working on the Hana sugar plantation. Boardinghouse meals were shared at the same table with Tokutaro Okada and his wife, Tsuru. Best of all was the steaming Japanese furo tub bath, under the tin roof outside. Large enough for two, the furo was a stimulating reprieve from a day's walking in the rain, a common event in Hana, and cuddling warmly in the hot tub a curiously erotic experience while the afternoon rain continued its loud beat on the roof overhead. Seemingly in accompaniment, a nearby diesel power plant generator intruded upon the rain sounds with a steady roar.

◁ On Captain Cook's return to Hawaii from his unsuccessful search for a northwest passage, he first anchored offshore at Pauwalu Point, where a young ali'i named Kamehameha rowed out to a meeting with the English explorer on his third and fatal voyage into the Pacific.

We hiked across old weed-choked sugarcane fields, slowly being replanted in Pangola range grass by the new landowner, San Francisco industrialist Paul Fagan, and often stopped for sweets at the Portuguese bakery, located in a small white cottage on the block where Hotel Hana-Maui would soon be constructed. Fagan built the hotel to house his own baseball team, the San Francisco Seals, the first of his many projects for the Hana community

Fagan built the Hana-Ranch hotel on the same land where Hana's Congregational missionaries constructed their first thatched huts for native worship, later moving across the road into the present church. In 1877 the American Board of Missions sold the unused property to Hana Plantation for $500. Cane was planted on the plot and narrow gauge railroad tracks laid across the field to carry sugarcane from the upland mill to cargo ships waiting in Hana Bay. In 100 years, the square block was estimated to be worth several million dollars to Hana Ranch.

The rocky shore beyond Hana town—
a place for walking alone.

Fifteen years later, I returned again to Hana, this time driving myself over the narrow, potholed Hana Road; stopped again at the same general stores enroute, sampled sweets and soda, and which was habitual with anyone driving the Hana Road, did not finally arrive until late in the afternoon when the green pastures were dark in the shadow from Haleakala. It was twilight when I finally finished pitching my tent in the Hana Bay Beach Park, shared Primo beer and fish with local people also camped on the beach, and drove uphill to Hotel Hana-Maui for dinner.

The next morning I looked around town. Okada store was gone. Weeds flourished among broken foundation bricks. The entire row of false-front shops along the makai (ocean) side of Hana's main street had disappeared. Only Hasegawa's store remained open on the mauka (mountain) side. The electric generating plant was eerily quiet, the iron building empty, replaced by a cross-country pole line carrying wires hill-to-hill all the way back to Kahului.

Every building was painted the same monotonous green. It was Fagan's idea. He would furnish the paint if everyone painted their own house and he gave everyone the same color. The Hasegawa store was no color—it hadn't been painted in years. Hotel Hana-Maui was an impeccably white stucco, looking very much like the luxury hotel it is. The large public rooms, added on by Fagan one after the other over the years, did not carry out any definite plan, yet the openness and informal atmosphere was quite appropriate to semitropical Hana. It was the first hotel I knew of without a front door.

Except for its green color, Hana had changed little in the fifteen years since I first walked there in the rain. Mostly, the changes were superficial—a rearranging of buildings, a few new items at Hasegawa's (although he already had most of everything), and a road sign at the highway junction into a town with no words—only an arrow pointing in each direction. The hotel was small, with only 100 or so guests in the spread-out rooms and cottages. They hardly intruded upon the casual Hana lifestyle enjoyed by residents, whose contact with visitors was mostly limited to hotel activities. Almost everyone worked for the hotel or for the ranch—daughters of cowboys were waitresses and their mothers were maids. It was a nice arrangement: the visitors in the exclusive hotel could feel superior and the Hana residents would ignore them all with impunity, yet many Hawaiians accepted hotel guests as friends and developed a warm relationship with them, while retaining their own impressive poise and self-respect.

I was to spend considerable time in the hotel after Fagan hired me to take photographs for promotion brochures and picture postcards. About once in twelve months I would make my way to Hana (in later years flying my own plane), unload a couple weeks' inventory of film, and move into the best room management had available to begin photography, rain or shine. It does rain in Hana, and the afternoon sun is a very brief event on the east side of Haleakala. It's a morning operation beginning at dawn, and if the sky is cloudy at dawn the day can be written off because nothing better will develop in the afternoon. Attempting to only photograph interiors does not solve the problem, for large sliding glass lanai doors require that the sun be shining brightly outside. Once on an early spring assignment I stayed an entire week at the hotel. It rained all day, everyday. I returned to Honolulu with only one useful photograph, which was made into a postcard that can probably still be purchased on the lobby rack. It's a picture of the hotel library and a good one, because I had a lot of time to work on it.

Hana is also where I go to be alone when I feel lonely. When I find it difficult to solve emotional events in an orderly manner, and it appears that a long walk by myself will provide opportunities to clear up conflicting desires, perhaps even cry a little. Hana is a good place to sift things out.

My usual walk begins just beyond the old Hana school, across from the ball park and makai of the hotel. A short road begins here and gradually disappears in the high grass near the barbed wire fence along an adjoining pasture. Jumping the fence into the cropped grass of the pasture is a leap into a simpler world, where perplexing problems proliferating in Honolulu become less and less intrusive.

The sun sets early in Hana and Haleakala's enormous hulk begins to cast a long shadow early in the afternoon, slowly spreading seaward like a flood of darkness. The shadow erases the harsh details of day, gradually changing the contrasting colors of the real world into more simple black and white shades of night. It is a good time and a good place to think of difficult things. Far out at sea, and in the sky overhead, daytime blue persists long after the scattered lights of Hana are turned on. They twinkle like stars as gentle onshore winds vibrate the leaves of trees between the nearest houses and me. Headlights of a car momentarily caress the hillside before blinking out around a curve in the Hana Road and the ocean surf, only moments before breaking against black lava rocks, now shatters in a void as the shape of rocks dissolves in the dark.

I've walked this shore on many long nights. Not walking far—that is unnecessary, for just being here is very far away. Sitting on a rock, leaning against a kamani tree, or lying on my back in the grass to see only the stars. Sometimes I fall asleep where I lie, smelling the salt in the air, cool ocean breezes barely felt on my face, the surf a slight whisper counterpointing the rustle of leaves overhead. The hard ground soon reminds me that I'm mortal, alive, and in need of a bed to be comfortable, so I slowly return to the lights and paved roads. But I always feel more composed, after an evening alone in Hana.

Except for hotel and magazine photography assignments, it was ten years before I returned to Hana for a lengthy stay, to write a book for Friends of the Earth, about Hana people and their unique rural lifestyle. Dave Brower was to eventually title the book *Maui: The Last Hawaiian Place*, a plea to leave things on East Maui the way they are.

I moved into Hana's first condominium, Hana Kai Resort, overlooking the Keanini surf in Hana Bay. The changes in Hana were the kind that don't show up on a casual visit; the consequences would not surface for several years. Hana Ranch and the hotel had new owners, a group of young Eastern mainlanders. The hotel's gardener had become ranch foreman, and after Fagan's death, his wife, Helene, donated a community hall on Hana Bay to the people of Hana and erected a huge cross on the highest cinder cone overlooking Hana that could be seen for miles in both directions. The road sign at the entrance to town, with arrows pointing in both directions, now had words indicating where the arrows pointed to.

Still, no television antennas could be seen. Not because there was any great disenchantment with the tube, but TV transmitters could not reach around the corner of Haleakala. Reception in Hana was all snow, but when a championship Maui high school team is playing off-island the entire town will be found in the cluster of cars parked at Hamoa, listening on portable TV sets. Hamoa is the nearest place to Hana that Big Island relay transmissions can be received without watching green people.

New homes for employees only, painted brown this time by management, had been constructed in a pasture across from the hotel, behind the fifty-year-old Hana Store, now the hotel laundry. Here and there along the road from Hana to Pu'uiki, wealthy mainland visitors purchased acreage on ranchlands and several apparently vacant plots without clear title, to build expensive, architect-designed homes, creating haole islands amidst the East Maui cow pastures.

The community was growing, but hardly changing. The low ratio of grazing white-faced Herefords to people varied little and continued to be an accurate way of measuring the Hana kind of living place. New residents increased, building a second home on Maui so they, too, would absorb some of the delightful rural environment, while at the same time innocently importing their own inadvertently corrosive traits. They joined together with cowboys, road workers, and hotel waitresses to discourage damaging urban improvements in an unusual citizen coalition to prevent dangerous encroachments upon the fragile land of East Maui.

On an early morning scouting walk for picture possibilities along O'heo Stream, where the mountain water from Kipahulu slips into the last pool and then into the ocean, I noticed several flagged stakes driven into the flat grassy area above the stream bank. They were survey stakes I hadn't seen before, delineating several connected rectangular spaces and looking suspiciously like a house site. It didn't take long to decide what to do. I pulled each stake out and threw them all into the ocean.

Who of the new mainland visitors was planning to build a house on O'heo Stream? Who would directly threaten the public right of access and the scenic integrity of Kipahulu Valley by building their home at Seven Pools? No matter how beautifully designed it might be, the action would be a desecration. I was outraged. Quickly writing an article for *Paradise* magazine, I warned the friends of Seven Pools that they should visit again soon for it may be the last time their children would be able to swim and play in O'heo Stream if the surveyor should return and replace the stakes. The editors published my plea in the next issue.

Sam Pryor, a retired vice president of Pan Am, phoned me shortly afterward. It was his house, but he had no intention of banning children from swimming in O'heo. I told him there was no way he could build a private home at Seven Pools and still allow the public in, that he must build elsewhere and sell his land back to whomever he bought it from. Within the month, Sam Pryor exchanged his Oʻheo land for a new house site by a waterfall he found on the other side of Kipahulu. He then encouraged Laurence Rockefeller to purchase the fifty-odd acres, including the popular Seven Pools, to remove the land permanently from the marketplace. For awhile we were worried that Rockefeller might build a luxury hotel on acreage bordering Kukui Bay adjacent to Oʻheo, but he decided to build his Mauna Kea Beach Hotel on the Big Island.

I was always somewhat disappointed that I had not seen the other waterfall before Sam found it. He told me of crawling on his hands and knees beneath a haʻo jungle maze to discover the replacement waterfall. At a dinner served in the gazebo canti/levered over his own stream, with spotlights directed on his personal waterfall, I enjoyed the carefully broiled steak while looking enviously at the hidden waterfall. It would have made a nice addition to a future national park.

Bumping along the lower Kipahulu pasture in Sam's four-wheel-drive Land Rover, which he generously loaned me so I might carry photographic equipment more easily into hard-to-get-to-to-places, I saw another vehicle approaching head on, from directly across the pasture. We continued toward each other, moving jerkily on the rough pasture until we stopped about fifty yards apart, facing each other. I was sure, whoever they were, that they were thinking as I was, wondering who is this person driving across the private Kipahulu Cattle Company ranch?

The other driver stepped out. He was tall, wide-shouldered, with an instantly recognizable grin spread across his tanned face. Charles Lindbergh was my childhood idol. I had read and reread *We* countless times, and he now walked across the pasture toward me as I, too, stepped out to greet him. His wife, Anne Morrow Lindbergh, small and fragile in appearance, rushed up to his side as I extended my hand. We greeted each other warmly, quickly discovering our common environmental concerns and agreement that all of Kipahulu must eventually become national park lands to prevent commercial exploitation.

I was never able to completely relax when talking with Lindbergh. I was awed in his presence, and I think Lindbergh sensed this on one occasion when he learned I was a pilot and flew my own Cessna 175A in Hawaii. Lindbergh asked me ,"What is it like flying a single-engine plane between the islands?" I had no idea how to reply to this pilot who was first to fly alone across the Atlantic, sometimes only fifty feet above the waves! Lindbergh followed with another question, "Do you fly high enough to glide between the islands if the engine fails?" I was mumbling something about the reliability of modern aircraft engines when he broke into a broad grin at my obvious discomfort. The following week I received an autographed copy of *We,* containing drawings and photographs of the "Spirit of St. Louis." Lindbergh was still my idol and he knew it.

Lindbergh later wrote to me about the magnificence of Maui. It became the introduction to my first Maui book, and expressed well the concern of an international conservationist. He said to me, "What balance between good and evil our civilized ways will bring, we cannot now foretell; but experience shows that they destroy unprotected wilderness and wild life with appalling ruthlessness; and that, unlike man's civilizations, destroyed nature cannot be rebuilt. Once violated it is gone forever, as is the ancient beauty of Waikiki Beach."

Charles Lindbergh returned to Kipahulu eight days before he died. United Airlines pilot William Picune flew the aviation pioneer home to Hawaii on a non-stop flight from New York City, with Lindbergh's stretcher positioned in the place of several rows of removed seats on the left side of the jet airliner so he would be able to see from the windows on his last ocean flight. As they neared the Hawaiian islands, the airline captain asked Lindbergh if he would like to circle the island of Maui. Lindbergh replied, "No, captain. I don't want to inconvenience the other passengers."

A rancher from Texas purchased the beautiful pastures of lower Kipahulu Valley, intending to subdivide the ranchland into commercial and residential lots. It was about this time that Governor John Burns appointed me to the Hawaii State Land Use Commisson, charged by the legislature with zoning all the land in the state and regulating its use. At an early meeting I asked my fellow commissioners to zone all of Kipahulu Valley into the Conservation District to halt this speculative urban development.

Jean McCaughey, owner of Kipahulu, wrote me personally, arguing that I was confiscating her land without due process; that she had every right to do what she wanted with her land, and had paid a high price with the intention of subdividing and selling the land. In a friendly exchange of letters, I replied contrariwise. Under Hawaii's state constitution we had the legal right to restrict the use of her property to preserve unique scenic resources. I was able to convince the reluctant commissioners that at least all the land makai of the highway must be conservation zoned, with mauka pasture lands zoned agriculture. It was duly voted unanimously.

Camped 8,000 feet above the wilderness floor of Kipahulu Valley on Kalapawili Ridge, an extension of the north rim of Haleakala Crater. The wonderfully soft grass is a native, tufted sedge, difficult for walking, but quite pleasant for sleeping.

During the next two years, Jean's philosophical attitude towards her Kipahulu land changed substantially and she eventually agreed that all of Kipahulu should become public land and be part of the national park. Sam Pryor and others had already acquired small parcels and built homes. It was too late to include these lands in the park; but with the help of Jean's ranch broker husband, Hamilton McCaughey, and the Nature Conservancy, who raised purchase funds on the mainland, Kipahulu Valley subsequently became an extension of Haleakala National Park. It was a personal pleasure to park at O'heo Bridge and see for the first time a uniformed park ranger watching over *our* land. Almost out of sight under the false kamani trees nearby, were two identical plastic lua huts, one labeled "men," the other "women." They were painted a strange brown color like all the other national park outhouses. Kipahulu was at last protected within the park, but we would no longer be able to relieve ourselves like before—just anywhere behind a tree.

Kipahulu residents have no Maui Electric Company meters on their homes. The power lines from Kahului go no further than Doctor Milton Howell's cliffside home in Pu'uiki. It's where a sign warns motorists, "baby pigs crossing." Some residents probably would like to receive light bills rather than be involved in the bother of generating their own electricity, but there are no power poles across Wailua Valley and along the road into Kipahulu because one resident definitely thought otherwise.

He was at the Kahului offices of the power company when a clerk asked him to check several right-of-way entry requests being prepared. The company wanted to clear-cut a thirty-foot swath through the Wailua Valley forest and needed permission to make surveys of the intended route. The resident kept his cool with difficulty, and asked to see all the survey requests. When they had been placed before him, he proceeded to rip each document into small pieces, until the entire file was waste paper. There still is no power line into Kipahulu.

Meanwhile, on top of the mountain, a bumbling superintendent of Haleakala National Park was telling hunters they couldn't shoot the goats that were busy chewing up every native grass and bush in sight. He would not compromise, saying only that "hunting was not permitted in national parks." I thought he was being silly and told him so. The feral goats had no natural enemy and should be eradicated. The last straw for me was his decision to remove the cast iron stoves from crater cabins because it was too expensive to carry in wood by mule. He would replace them with butane stoves, and eliminate one of the great delights of overnight stays in Haleakala—the rare opportunity of cooking on top of an old-fashioned, wood-burning stove. It is an integral part of the crater experience, and a butane burner is not a suitable substitute. He was adamant, however, and refused to consider alternate, more inexpensive ways of bringing firewood into the crater of Haleakala.

With the help of Sam Pryor, I obtained an appointment with Walter Hickel, then Secretary of the Interior, and took the next jet with an empty seat to Washington, D.C. Hickel proved to be very understanding when I explained the problem, and gave me none of the expected bureaucratic excuses. After our meeting, where we also discussed boundaries for the new Kipahulu section, he directed me down the hall, where there had been arranged a meeting with the national park director.

He asked me the hard question. If I didn't like the superintendent now on the job, what kind of a superintendent did I want? I gulped, not having a ready answer, but was eventually able to describe the kind of superintendent we needed on Maui, the kind who would get off his mountaintop ivory tower, move down to sea level with us ordinary people, and reasonably implement regulations, not just quote them like inflexible dogma. When I arrived back on Maui the offending superintendent had already left the islands. They still use wood in the crater stoves.

To photograph upper Kipahulu Valley for *National Geographic* magazine, I chartered a Bell Ranger helicopter to drop me off on the valley rim so I might easily walk into the edge of wilderness at the back of Kipahulu. I had a tight deadline and insufficient time to backpack all the way into Haleakala. The helicopter would do it quickly, and also enable me to fly in a good friend for a crater visit. George Treichel, professor at San Francisco State University, was visiting in Hawaii and I knew he would like to see Haleakala. He was crippled by polio and unable to walk without crutches. I called him in Honolulu and suggested he meet the helicopter in Hana for a lift into the crater and an experience otherwise impossible.

Are the whales in love? Does the male whale sing to his female when mating? Scientists swim with the humpback whale in Lahaina waters to find out. Cataloging individual whales by patterns of pigmentation, scars, and scratches acquired in their travels, the scientists hope to learn how long the whales stay in Maui and what they're doing—mating, calving, or singing; traveling from north to south and back, for fun or some yet unknown serious purpose. They have recorded males singing when they join females and during mating, and the interaction between groups

GREGG SILBER

JIM DARLING

72

of whales. The humpback whale's intelligence and purposive lifestyle have become a fascinating discovery, and whales visiting Maui have been found as far north as the Gulf of Alaska and south below Baja, Mexico. During the winter months, from December through May, Maui is the assembling place for some 500 humpback whales, mating and giving birth to their young, before moving on to food-rich northern seas. These photographs by Maui scientists were taken under special research permits issued for the New York Zoological Society, sponsor of their research.

JIM DARLING

JIM DARLING

We met as arranged and George was dropped off in the meadow near Paliku cabin, where we would spend the night. I flew on to Kipahulu for the day. George found it boring just sitting around the cabin, and decided to hobble out on his aluminum crutches along the main crater trail for half-a-mile or so. He was well out of sight of the cabin when along came a group of tired, dusty hikers, a full day's walk from the trail's start about nine miles back. George moved aside on his crutches so they could pass on the trail. No one said a word, but each hiker looked back after passing, obviously not believing what he saw.

Hiking and camping is my pleasure-time activity, fitting in perfectly with working photography and, in terms of past experiences, providing a very useful bank of research data on the way places were. I have been virtually everywhere in the state of Hawaii, driving every road—paved and unpaved—climbing to every mountaintop, and camping on every beach I could conveniently locate. I've hiked every trail the Hawaiian Trail and Mountain Club scheduled, and blazed a few others I got lost on.

My first camping trip into Haleakala was in 1947. We started the tramp at Olinda, above Haiku, hiking to the summit rim with one overnight in a cave enroute, several more days in the crater cabins and then downhill through Kaupo Gap to the shore. We continued walking on around East Maui to Hana, joining the Koʻolau Ditch at Kipiliʻili Falls and walking the long ditch trail almost back to Haʻiku where we began. We shared pack loads equally, utilizing the time-honored backpacker method of having the person who sorted each day's load take the last apportionment as his own.

My load for most of the trip was a single round of American cheese. If I remember correctly, it was about two feet in diameter and despite the fact that hunks were sliced out for blending with eggs at breakfast, nibbling at lunch, and melting with macaroni at dinner, every mile on the trail seemingly made the heavy cheese heavier. Hikers following me on the trail said the slowly increasing size of the triangular gap was an excellent way to measure our progress. When the cheese was half gone—we would be near Hana.

Walking is considerably more informative than driving. It is unnecessary to look where you're going—you look at what you see, talk to it if it talks, and argue with it if it talks back. Visual images last longer and are remembered more accurately. There is time to consider and make judgment, to smell the flowers, touch a rock, sense the temperature, or feel the texture of a leaf. Time is ample around a campfire at day's end to share these experiences and perhaps to even embroider them a little, add color to the drab, and then separate chaff from the wheat so as to better perceive the reality. On the trail you can look back where you've been.

Walking on top of Maui is a good place to think of islands because they can all be seen. On the crater rim of Haleakala at Red Hill, 10,023 feet above everything, the Big Island's high volcanic mountains protrude above the tradewind cloud layer south of Maui; due west is Kahoʻolawe beyond tiny Molokini; northwest is Lanaʻi, and Molokaʻi, and beyond them can be seen Oʻahu on a clear day. Only Kauaʻi is out of sight below the horizon. West Maui is like an island of its own, rising gracefully from the green sugarcane blanketing flat central Maui, encircled by a doughnut cloud resting on the afternoon tradewind's inversion layer.

On assignment for *Life* magazine, I photographed West Maui by the light of an H-bomb shot into the ionosphere in the nose cone of a Thor rocket launched from Johnston Island, 800 miles west of Maui. It was on the sixth night of my driving up and down Haleakala, for each of the previous countdowns were aborted and I returned to my room in the old Wailuku Hotel with no photographs to show for hours of waiting in the cold. One test was canceled because two Air Force Hasselblad cameras jammed. I fixed them the next day (I used the same type of cameras for my advertising work), returned to the summit, and waited. My shortwave radio monitored the countdown from Johnston, and nuclear testing agency scientists advised me on calculations for the exposure, as it would hardly be possible to use a light meter. My array of 35 mm tripod-mounted Canon cameras was arranged in the direction pointed out to me, but one camera was aimed in the direction of West Maui. I thought it would be fascinating to photograph the island lighted by the flash of an H-bomb.

The Thor rocket was off its pad and rising after the count of zero. I carefully set all my shutters on "time." There was no sound on the dark mountain as I waited for the night to end. Suddenly the sky, sea, and earth were wiped out in a brilliant white glare that hurt my eyes. The H-bomb had detonated.

Just as suddenly as there was light there was darkness, but now all the stars were gone. The blackness seemed to push in against me, when a bright green star rapidly appeared where none existed before and, with horrible swiftness, grew monstrously into an exploding ball of fire—800 miles away and 240 miles above me, yet at arm's length. I didn't want to reach out.

The smaller of the two Wai'anapanapa Ponds, almost 8,000 feet high on the north rim of Haleakala in an 'ohi'a lehua forest eight miles above Hana town. No trails enter the forest; the hidden ponds are cool swimming holes available only to those hikers willing to search and find them in the tropical jungle.

The silent light changed in seconds from green to bloody red, then spread its stain irresistibly across space, polluting the heavens in the afterbirth of a hydrogen bomb. Only then did the stars hesitantly reappear to twinkle again in the unreal bloody sky, now in competition with high-energy electrons stimulated in the earth's magnetic field, actually bending it out of shape as we learned later. Graceful arcs glowed across the horizon, creating an artificially induced aurora borealis shimmering around Maui in the momentary eternity before the heavens stopped bleeding.

I quietly closed the shutter on each camera, packed everything in its proper case, and drove down the twisting Haleakala Road to Kahului Airport, arriving long after midnight. I located my plane on the ramp, took off into the dark sky, and without thinking much of anything—but with lots of thoughts on my mind—flew directly to Honolulu, where I transferred my film to a New York bound jet, meeting *Life's* rapidly closing deadline.

My bloody sky was printed full-page in next week's issue, but not my "flash" picture of Maui. Not until sometime later when I was able to search through my slide rejects did I find it. The picture looked like any ordinary picture taken in the sunlight—blue ocean and white surf, green cane fields, white clouds in a blue sky. The picture was not usable in *Life,* because it looked like any other picture—the exposure was absolutely perfect.

Beyond Kipahulu, the highway around East Maui becomes an unpaved track along the shore—splashed by ocean waves during stormy weather and in places completely washed away by raging streams.

Maui politics is somewhat like dunking for apples. About the time you locate fruit it skitters away out of reach, yet loyalty is lasting and discretion a fine-honed virtue. Who you are and what you have is important, yet simply knowing your way through the political maze does not, in itself, produce results. Payoffs and an occasional bribe undoubtedly occur, but campaign funds from businessmen are generally spread around quite evenly. Sierra Club activists say the county is developer-oriented. Contractors claim the government's orderly growth policy is halting construction of needed hotels. One of the largest developers working on Maui had his building permit for an 800-room hotel held up by the Mayor for an entire year until he was able to arrange for construction of low-cost housing for hotel employees. After I described Maui County as a "license bureau for developers," now-retired Mayor Elmer Cravalho wouldn't speak to me for an entire year. Maui politics are probably not much different from anywhere else. It's just that they occur on a small island and it's difficult to cover awkward aberrations. Most political observers have heard of the copious gifts proffered political appointees, of opulent hospitality—wild game birds, abundant drinks, expensive brandy, even a girl for the evening. As a Land Use Commissioner, I learned all this was true, and not necessarily limited to corporate landowners. The small property owner was just as desirous of making the commissioner's life a happy one.

Influence is considered to be an important ingredient in obtaining a zoning change, more important than just asking. In over three years as commissioner I never bought a drink on Maui. Somehow the drink I ordered, no matter where, was paid for when it was time to pay the check. There was always a friendly developer sitting over in the corner. One of my concerns was that no conservationist ever bought me a drink to help make things even.

We ignored most of the influence peddlers and went on to some very credible achievements. The basic conclusions of this early commission, in designating all the land, public and private, as conservation, agricultural, rural, and urban, is still on the maps in substantially the same way we drew the boundaries eighteen years ago. Urban districts containing tourist destination areas have changed little. The several urban strips from Wailea to Kapalua developed as we expected, restricting most Maui hotels and condos to the dry west shore, where scenic values would not be compromised by planned development. The kiawe wilderness of Wailea, a recent introduction of its own, was replaced with coconut palms and golfing grass. The resort developers paid to bring water into Wailea, where warm sun and miles of beaches guaranteed private multimillion-dollar investments. While the tourist industry built some 17,000 transient rooms in fifteen years, over 90 percent of Maui Island remained unchanged in conservation, agricultural, and rural land use districts. At Wailea, there are only two hotels, with less than 1,000 rooms between them. A third hotel of 300 rooms will probably be the last in an area three times the size of Waikiki.

One of my first confrontations after Kipahulu was over the petition by a large corporate landowner wanting to change the zoning of his oceanside land from conservation to urban so he would have more flexibility in planning the location of hotel and condominium units. I viewed the request as a desire to exclude local residents, to even keep out pole fishermen wanting to fish the rocky shore. The landowner told me privately that this was so, but that I should understand his problem. Noisy beer parties on the beach at all hours would severely inhibit sales of expensive condos. The public must be excluded from the beaches, as they are at Ka'anapali, where there are no public rights-of-way between hotels.

I opposed this approach to resort development on Maui and was determined to use whatever influence I possessed to expand public access to privately owned shorelands. I could not understand why anyone would be disturbed over an occasional beach party. Wasn't this the kind of informal island lifestyle that everyone wanted to share in? I had been invited to join a few raucous beach parties over the years and while they were noisy, the Primo beer was always cold, the Hawaiian music inventive, and the girls friendly. As I looked at the problem, the only matter to worry about was whether you were invited or not. The beaches were ours. We would lose them to the tourists unless public rights-of-way were given to us by the affected property owner. Just as we argued at Kipahulu, the property owner did not have the right to use his land contrary to the long-term best interests of ordinary citizens.

A master plan was prepared for Hana, calling for the moving of resident shopping away from the town center and the restricting of hotel employee homes to the outskirts of town. At the ensuing public hearing in the Helene Community Hall there was considerable opposition. I described the unwise proposals as an inept attempt to create a "haole tourist ghetto." The plan was never heard of again.

There were no environmentally concerned organizations on Maui thirty years ago. Today there must be fifty, including community and business clubs that rapidly became involved when growing tourist industry activities began to conflict with local assumptions about public uses never before challenged. Developers suddenly faced an aroused public in the early sixties, and responded with some of the worst and some of the finest resort planning in the world.

From a cultural environmentalist's point of view, the most spectacular example of responsive resort planning, Maui style, must be the hotel-condo complex of Wailea. The old coast road was moved inland from the popular Wailea beaches to provide space for new hotels on the valuable beach frontage. In the spaces between the three hotel sites, short public roads to the separate beaches were constructed, with paved parking areas and turn-around culs-de-sac. Beach access to the public was more convenient than ever. It could have been planned by an environmentalist.

Fishermen park their cars in the Kapalua Hotel parking lot and walk out on rocky Hawea Point for a day's fishing. Overlooking their fishing holes are half-million dollar condominiums. Following the example set at Wailea, the public at Kapalua Beach also enjoy their own separate parking lot, a short distance from possibly the finest swimming beach on West Maui, a beach they share with guests at nearby Kapalua Hotel.

Thirty-five years after my first honeymoon I again returned to Hana. The remote village at first evidenced little change. The Kinoshita Store foundation was filled in and paved—transformed into a parking lot for Hasegawa General Store, still selling almost everything anyone needed. Most of the bearded and unkempt hippies from ten years ago were missing, but it was no longer permissible to camp at Hana Bay, and ranch gates, previously left open for anyone wishing to cross the pasture to a favorite fishing hole, were now locked. Walking across the Hana Ranch pasture was trespassing, but the Kipahulu Ranch gates were open to anyone—the cattle grazed on national park lands. (Be careful where you step and sit down to picnic.) The mauka Hana Airport lands were subdivided, and a new Hana school occupied rocky makai pasture lands half way into town.

At Hotel Hana-Maui, I did note a more disturbing change. In the dining room, which for thirty years had been staffed exclusively with local Hawaiian girls—where daughters of waitress mothers would return to work at the hotel—I found myself ordering dinner from a blonde mainland haole girl. She was pleasant, attractive, perhaps even more efficient than the Hana girls who for so many years claimed this hotel as their own domain. What had happened? I asked a familiar Hawaiian face at the next table. Where had everyone gone? She replied softly, ''We don't like working here anymore.''

Later that same evening I walked down to Hana Bay to see what changes might have taken place on the beach road. Approaching a group of Hawaiians drinking beer around a park picnic table, I voiced a friendly hello, but received no encouragement to join them. I walked on, overhearing derogatory remarks about haole tourists.

I wish I could visit Hana for the first time. Perhaps it might then be possible to place undesirable events in a clearer perspective, to erase emotional events I have colored in pastel shades because I want to see them pleasantly. I don't want to see harsh, conflicting colors of unpleasant events challenging my memories of our island world. I'm too much of an optimist to remember otherwise, like the time I was driving along the Kawela shore on Moloka'i and stopped to watch a hukilau, taking pictures of the fishermen hauling in their nets filled with flopping fish. Unexpectedly, a fisherman reached out to hand me a fish, saying they had enjoyed having me take their picture! I took the fish over to the Midnight Inn in Kaunakakai where it was cooked for dinner. I ordered the ''seafood special'' on the menu— mine.

There have been changes. There was the time when you could dredge your own clams out of Kupeke fishpond with a hoe for fifty cents a bucket, and sail from Honolulu to Kahului on the deck of an inter-island steamer for $5 overnight (steerage fare). I remember chartering an entire DC-3 aircraft from Aloha Airlines for $150 an hour. With thirty friends in the Hawaiian Trail and Mountain Club sharing the cost, I would organize flying weekend camping trips to the outside islands. We took as long as possible to get there, using all the gas in the plane, standing behind the pilot and telling him where we wanted to go. Once we flew up inside Pelekunu Valley below the clouds touching the mountaintops, across the saddle and back out Wailau Valley in the rain, loooking at the waterfalls straight on. Or flying with a dozen friends in our airplanes over to Lana'i Airport and holding our own airshow for the day—taking off side by side, and having our flour-bag bombing contest interrupted only once by a commercial airliner wanting to land on schedule. And stopping on the way from Hilo to Honolulu at Moloka'i Airport to steal pineapples off the west end of the runway. You can't do these things anymore.

Lahaina's Front Street is today a stroll along half a hundred storefronts of jewelry: there's even a ''ring lady'' to make what hasn't already been made. This year is the jewelry phase of Lahaina. Next year may be something else. Four years ago it was puka puka shells; five years ago, the mu'umu'u; fifteen years back it was cotton Tahitian prints. At one time there were four or five fabric shops in Lahaina; now there are none, as merchants respond to changing tastes of the tourists. The days when the visitor's first Hawaiian purchase was a mu'umu'u may be gone—even local residents are not wearing the shapeless body cover like years ago, when the mu'umu'u at home was de rigueur.

The commerical Lahaina is rather inviting to the unwary investor. Its main street and interior courts are littered with empty windows, closed doors, and the remains of broken dreams. There appears to be a limitless market, with the sidewalks crowded with tan bodies and credit cards looking for a gift to take home. The apparent business opportunities can be irresistible to those searching for a pleasant retirement; so they lease a small shop, hang out their sign, and stock a batch of seashells from the Philippines, gold chains from Hong Kong, black coral from Maui—and open the door. After six to nine months their savings will be gone. One storefront has seen seven new businesses in eight years; a turnover in Lahaina that is commonplace, especially among mom-and-pop stores opened by visitors without retail experience or an accurante knowledge of the tourist market. The people walking up and down the streets of Lahaina are mostly "just looking," traveling on coupons without cash to spend on impulse items. At the Lahaina McDonald's they sit at familiar tables, splitting a hamburger for lunch. "Gee, honey, I sure would like a beer." "Well, is it on the coupon?" Serving visitors with fatter wallets from an incredible menu, which included buffalo steaks, roast tiger, deer, antelope, and snake, a fancy candle-lit restaurant on Front Street went out of business the same year it opened—before anybody could object. Up the block, Lahaina's Hawaiian Wax Museum closed its doors, selling its wax images of historical Hawaii that visitors refused to pay to see: plastic bamboo decorations were $4 a bunch, rope rigging from a fake whaling ship $5, and Olympic swimming champion Duke Kahanumoku's real surfboard $3,500 marked down from $8,000.

With gradually rising airfares, tour groups are decreasing, replaced by more affluent independent travelers. There are more children and families, especially during winter months, a sure sign it is becoming more expensive to travel; working-class people seldom bring their children—the upper middle-class always do. Visitors are buying half-million-dollar condominiums at Kapalua and moving in themselves, and hundreds more come back at least once a year to check on their rental investment and spend a few days in Maui's sun. These are people who can go to Olah's Shop and buy a jade bracelet, who will shop at The Gallery, buy a Maui artist's oil and eat, and drink at the Blue Max. They are doing well. It is the curio shop selling shell beads for thirty-nine cents that is fading away, but the business opportunities still remain. A restaurant was recently offered for sale—asking price: one million dollars.

Neither Lahaina, Hana, nor Maui is the place it was. Hana was originally a small sugar town, then a cowtown, then a rural town with a hotel. Hana is now a small place of no particular description and of no age, in danger of being subdivided and overrun with tourists. If you loved the old Hana you may not like the new unless you are ready to accept the changes constantly occurring on Maui—changes that have been underway since the Polynesians first settled on these islands. Or you may be able to see Hana and Maui for the first time and not be aware of any changes. All of Maui is like that, becoming something new; like the people from all the other places, the protea and ginger flowers from other worlds, the cultures and languages melding into something called the "island way." It's all the new Maui.

I have walked for thirty-five years on Maui, actively participating in island life with island people, helping nourish the growth of cultural and political activists to build a better living place. I have always felt that our interracial community must be the envy of the world. What was happening in Hana that placed our island world in jeopardy? Was the harmonious relationship of people from everywhere just something I wanted to see, something that hid a less desirable view of our island people? I hardly felt that to be so; but as I talked with others, it was clear that too many tourists driving into Hana had turned the people of Hana against the haole visitor. Over 300 rental cars had been counted crossing the O'heo Bridge one day last summer. Hana residents were being crowded out of their own backyard, and soon the national park was being criticized for turning Seven Pools into a place for tourists.

Conflict between native Hawaiians and visitors is nothing new. It began with the first haole visitor to Hawaii, the British explorer Captain James Cook, who was killed in a cultural disagreement over property rights. The Hawaiians said everyone owned the longboat they had taken from Cook's ship—Cook said the boat was his exclusively. The missionaries introduced racial discrimination and the concept of private property; visiting whalers and traders imported deadly diseases; planters brought in sugar, alien plantation labor, and then overthrew the Hawaiian monarchy. It is understandable that native Hawaiians would occasionally display a little animosity directed against the haole. It helps little to argue that the immigrant people to these islands have created in Hawaii a democratic community, with human rights and economic opportunities second to none. As they did with mainland Indians, the haoles took the land and established on it the greatest nation on earth.

More than 350 persons crowded into Hana's Helene Community Hall to meet with Hawaii's Lieutenant Governor Jean King and talk about the tourist "problem" and the National Park Service condemnation of native Hawaiian lands to expand the park in Kipahulu Valley. The mostly Hawaiian audience was hostile and obviously did not like what was happening in Hana.

The Kahoʻolawe ʻOhana activist, Dr. Emmet Aluli, flew in from Molokaʻi to protest, saying his family had learned they owned an interest in one of the Kipahulu parcels being condemned. Aluli said, "We didn't know we owned the land, until we saw the legal advertisements where our name was listed along with a hundred others with possible undivided interest claims." He added that his family "had started a kitty to raise money to fight the condemnation and wasn't interested in the $1,500 an acre the government was offering. We're not after the money. If this land belongs to our family, it should stay in the family. The federal government has got plenty of land already."

Ann Trask Gibson, adding her legal voice to the discussion, claimed the parcels were being condemned so they could be turned over to the National Park Service, but that they "belong to native Hawaiian landowners who still exist today; they are very much alive." She said if these owners stuck together the government "would back off."

Others changed the subject for awhile and asked for a gym and library for Hana. Complaints about the Hana Road potholes were numerous until the lieutenant governor said, "I'm really getting the message on the road, you know." Mary Pinho said, "I think many of us will be down under before the road is fixed." When a visitor from Honolulu told the meeting, "Why don't you people get together and make the Hana Road straight?" he was answered with loud boos. Elmer Ching said, "If you talk about a straight highway, you're going to get into a lot of trouble with the people of Hana. We don't want any freeway coming into Hana." He sat down to solid applause.

The restless group was also asked if it favored expanding the parking area at Seven Pools from 80 to 120 stalls and the crowd erupted in no-no-no, and when they were asked if the parking should be kept at 80 stalls, there were calls to make it 40. Mary Pinho commented that "park superintendent Huntzinger is here and he has heard us loud and clear."

The crowd grew unruly, began interrupting speakers and referring to park expansion as a rip-off. Doctor Milton Howell, the only physician for thirty miles in either direction and a long-time advocate of the park at Kipahulu, objected to the meeting announcement written by Hawaiian activists, saying it was "a vicious letter accusing people of stealing and lying," adding that he "was one of them. We worked very hard a few years back through the Nature Conservancy in order to buy the land and turn it over to the National Park Service. I don't believe that it is necessary to hurt people who didn't have a crystal ball to see the condos coming and rental cars in Hana by the thousands. Those who worked to acquire the new park extension that has resulted in the present proceedings to clear title to seven parcels had no ulterior motive."

Skippy Young rose to make what I thought to be a very reasonable motion. He demanded that the National Park Service "sit down with the Hana people and draw up some kind of satisfactory proposal agreeable to the National Park Service and the community of Hana." Howell agreed, saying he supported the motion, noting that "many compromises can be made. If we had not bought this land there would be a big 'no trespassing' sign on it and none of us could go on it."

I had been thinking about what I would say for the past half hour. The aggravated audience recognized me, sitting in the back of the room, and being the outspoken pro-park activist I was, I'm sure they were convinced I would oppose the motion. It was time to stand up. I raised my hand to be recognized and began making my way to the front of the room. The hall fell silent as I walked. Muffled remarks about me could be heard as I neared the microphone.

"I'm speaking in favor of the motion." There was sustained applause throughout the hall, as I, too, asked the park service to again "get down off the mountain," and sit down and talk with the people of Hana. It was the right thing to say at the right time, and I could not suppress a satisfying grin on my face all the way back to my seat. I felt good. I felt like a Hawaiian.

Lieutenant Governor Jean King was all smiles. She had worried that her meeting might be disrupted; instead, a constructive resolution evolved. She spoke warmly of the "beautiful thing that happened this evening," and bid the audience aloha. As I left the hall, walking by the front platform to say goodnight, the lieutenant governor leaned over and kissed me. Things were still all right on Maui. □

| The pleasant fragrance of Hana Road is the fragrance of yellow ginger in the fall of the year.

Clear waters of Pailolo Channel hug the pleasant shore from Napili to Honokahua. At Kapalua Beach the adjacent elegant Kapalua Hotel mixes visitors with local people on a popular public beach, while in Namalu Bay, beyond the edge of the hotel's front lawn, swimming in private is a special kind of luxury.

In Kula country, averaging 3,000 feet above the central Maui cane fields, an abundant flora converts the drive into a botanical delight, somewhat reflective of Maui everywhere, but with greater variety. In the front yard of St. Joseph's Church a typical mix occurs: Norfolk Island pine; the flaying blossoms of a Mexican species of sisal displaying probably the longest known flower, and one of the 180 species of Aloe. Close up, (opposite page), the bird of paradise is like a roaring flame on the blade of a sword.

A complete list of Maui's flora would be another book. The incredible variety can only be hinted at in a sample of color, texture, and scale: red thimbleberries are a hiker's small, but delicious, snack on mountain trails; leaves from weedy ''air plants'' growing wild along rural roads can be mailed from Maui and thumbtacked to a mainland apartment wall, where they continue to grow; exotic red ginger likes it wet and shady; cultivated pineapple requires little water; bougainvillea grows in a hundred pastel shades and seems to require no care at all; the magnificent silversword is abundant in Haleakala crater, where the silver ball of swordlike leaves slowly emerges for ten years or so, then suddenly sends forth a long florescent shaft, at times six feet high with hundreds of blossoms. The silversword blooms once then dies.

Overleaf. On the floor of Haleakala, a winding cinder trail traverses the route to Paliku cabin. Rainfall variations inside the crater produce a change from desert to swamp in one day's walk. On the crater rim above Paliku a miniature lake, Wai'anapanapa, is hidden to all but the most adventurous hiker.

Winter waves challenge surfers at Kulaoka'e'a on the Maui shore beyond Kapalua. At sunset in the channel between Ka'anapali and Lana'i, canoe club racers practice for the Maui championship.

A rainy day on Maui. It's the same island, but the upland ranching town of Makawao and the ocean beach at Ka'anapali are worlds apart.

In the middle of the largest sugar plantation in Hawaii, Hawaiian Commercial and Sugar Company's Pu'unene mill is a familiar sight to visitors on arriving jetliners passing directly overhead on their approach to Kahului Airport. Sugar planters deliberately burn mature cane before the harvest to enhance sugar content and to rid the crop of unnecessary leaf trash.

3

About Living on the Maui Islands

The extraordinary tree growing abundantly almost everywhere on all the islands is called mesquite in Texas, where it seldom gets bigger than a bush, and kiawe in Hawaii, where it sometimes grows bigger than a house, with a trunk four feet across. The tree with the crooked, knock-kneed branches dropping nasty thorns to step on, seems to cover every place where nothing else wants to grow. It's not good for climbing—the branches bend down where they should go up. It's a pest and a bother to many who consider the tree not much more than an overgrown weed. I like it. It may be my favorite tree.

Whenever I have extra time on Maui, I drive to the end of the paved road at Wailea onto the dusty cinder road towards Makena and under the kiawe forest that extends from here on. At the end of the day or the end of the week, the kiawe wilderness of Makena offers a quick escape from the orderly part of Maui, the carefully manicured and mowed landscape of tourist resorts, where a few weeds would be desirable, and some occasional dirt positively delightful. It's good for the soul to be in a forest where the trees are not straight and the branches have no leaves to speak of.

Kiawe is not the kind of tree you walk under; where it is easy to pick up a branch of inch-long thorns capable of piercing clear through a leather shoe sole—or thin rubber slipper. Neither are kiawe good to look at; they are only good to look through, and at this they have no peer. Take the coconut. A grove of coconut trees is a forest of telephone poles. Or take the pink rainbow shower tree. When it's not showering, the branches don't know what to do. It's the most awkward tree found anywhere.

Stroll through the kiawe beyond Wailea's Hotel Intercontinental, being careful where you step, and watch the day go by overhead. In morning light the branches are gray, in the afternoon they become black silhouettes. At noon the canopy directly overhead is a bright glittering green, splayed into a lacework of tiny branches shaking in the slightest breeze. At the end of day, looking west through the crooked maze of kiawe branches, the sky is divided into an abstract masterpiece of pastel shades in late sunset color, blending gradually into dark when the sun disappears behind Lana'i. The experience is only a five-minute walk from one of the finest luxury hotels in Hawaii. A walk through weeds and thorns that provide the contrast and perspective necessary to appreciate the place we live. After all, a diet only of carefully mowed lawns and box-trimmed shrubs, where no one lets the coconuts mature and fall, would be mighty bland.

What I like about Wailea, as a resort, is that the place has the correct amount of kiawe trees and dirt. In a way, Wailea exemplifies why Maui Island itself is so enjoyable to so many. It's that dramatic mix of dirt and concrete, kiawe and coconut palm. Wailea provides the opportunity to be proper and self-confident when desired, offered side by side with a real possibility of stubbing your toe on a lava rock. Wailea beach is not an exclusive tourist preserve, but a place that mixes people who came to Maui generations ago and stayed with those just passing by for an hour in the sun. It's the sweet and sour combination served on a gourmet platter, with the wonderful discovery of tasting the entree without knowing who is the spice and who is the sugar. At Wailea it matters not from which end of the beach you come.

◁ Maui man, proud descendant of the first ocean navigators and discoverers of Hawaii, may today be a hotel musician or tour bus driver—or a doctor or lawyer. He loves the sea and the land. Hawaii is his personal possession.

In the old days, before A&B built its hotels, Wailea was my favorite beach for swimming in the nude. The sand is soft and the surf mostly gentle, and a short walk up the beach around a rocky ledge was far away from anybody. On moonlit nights the beach is particularly glorious, a circumstance that must not be chanced alone. Two is mandatory, and then the possibility for love should be welcome. It is like making love in Haleakala, where the sky is all around and there are only two people in the world—but be careful of the wet sand and kiawe thorns.

Designing Maui resorts is apparently a matter of deciding what to do with the kiawe trees. Amfac, which started Maui tourism on its way with its instantly successful Ka'anapali resort, began its project by moving back the state highway, cutting away most of the kiawe forest, and bulldozing everything else flat. Landscape architects then put it all back together again, planting trees without thorns where they would not interfere with hotels or drop leaves on the beach.

Someone at A&B must like kiawe, for they did Wailua my way. They started work by moving the state highway back, then building public right-of-way access culs-de-sac to the best beaches, carefully cleaning up while leaving the largest kiawe in place and locating the hotels so they would not interfere with the trees. From the very beginning, the financial partners at Wailea instructed management to treat the land with the respect it deserved—seeing in the rocky desert far more value than is at first evident.

A&B begins to clear the kiawe forest at Wailea in 1973, uncovering sand dunes and preparing the land for Maui's newest luxury resort. Golf course fairways and greens go in first.

In the early sixties, Amfac cleared away kiawe forest and caneland for its famous Ka'anapali resort. The oasis of coconut palms was planted in the sand before hotel construction began.

Wailea is very quiet. Nothing seems about to happen and probably won't. Wailea, like the symphony it is, must be participated in and carefully listened to. It is not elevator music. One of the best restaurants in Hawaii is at Wailea, Raffles; but to buy the tour bus driver's favorite, Primo beer, it is necessary to travel far north, to Laurence Rockefeller's hotel at Kapalua. Guests at Wailea seem to lie down more than they sit, and some honeymoon couples are up late dancing to the last disco note, yet arrive at breakfast for the first serving to get an early start on a drive around the island—the long way. Guests drink more gin and vodka than rum, but that would be expected in a resort where there are more rental cars than tour buses. Wailea is on the same side of the island as Ka'anapali, but very far away. It is nice to have both.

Ka'anapali is a very exciting place to be, always giving the definite impression that something might happen at any moment and probably will. Trams, tour buses, and taxis clutter up the entrance drives, while twin-engine commuter aircraft land and take off on the next-door landing strip. The highway carries a constant stream of traffic between Kahului and Kapalua, and five miles down the road is Lahaina, which by law is a town in a state of suspended animation. A steam ''sugarcane'' railroad shuttles passengers back and forth in a tourist environment created from scratch, where guests sit around a lot and honeymooners go to bed immediately after an early dinner and miss breakfast. The parking lots are full; the hotels are full, and have been since the first day. Ka'anapali is possibly one of the most popular resorts in the world, with one of the best beaches anywhere.

No other island has a Lahaina—Hawaii's curio store of people, all appearing very much at home because people mix very well together in Lahaina. Shopping in the numerous shops is not what makes Lahaina: it is the people who blend so well in the historical environment and are of such an incredible variety.

Lahaina attracts quiet, serious visitors delighted in the opportunity to let their hair down and open their shirt in the relaxed freedom of a resort town and, weird creatures of no known sex who materialize in the waterfront park at sunset to stare into space . . . Aboard tour boats and visiting pleasure craft are leather-skinned, blonde water people dressed perpetually in bikinis and shorts . . . Young mainlanders working in hotels for a year of surfing. . . . Unshaven construction workers stopping for a beer. All together with local west-side residents in town for dinner. Lahaina is an excellent place for watching people, the chance arrangement of old buildings and new architectural details offering a voyeur's promised land. In second-floor bars are plenty of railings to lean on, windows for looking out of, and places to sit, lean, or stand on in any corner.

Lahaina itself may be the best curio of all. Both sides of Front Street and 100 feet behind are part of Maui County historic districts 1 and 2, and a National Historic Landmark, one of the few in the U.S. with definite boundaries. On the makai side they extend one mile out to sea.

To build anything in Lahaina requires approval of the State Historic Preservation officer in Honolulu, and if the planned construction is along the shore, then coastal zone management approval is also necessary. Depending on what is being done a dozen permits may be required, with public hearings to determine possible public impacts. If adverse, an environmental impact statement will then be necessary. A recent building required two and a half years to finally get the go-ahead. One phase is easy; after the Maui Historic Commission takes action, it simply adjourns to meet as the Coastal Zone Management Commission. Both are the same people.

Historic district status for Lahaina at first generated considerable opposition from property owners wanting to demolish their historic buildings and build modern multistory condominiums along Front Street. The majority decided that was not the way, and waterfront land in Lahaina, now limited to 2-story structures, is worth more than some Waikiki lots with 37-story buildings on them. The historic district was established without help from any government agency; no government monies or HUD funds were used. The idea of urban renewal was never thought of—the idea in essence was not to renew the urban. Several building projects were denied in the early years; but now, when developers want to build, they first visit the historic commission, hat in hand, saying, ''I want to build a restaurant,'' or whatever, and ask them how to do it. The historical concept has become so profitable, builders even ask what size the windows should be, how many panes, and what color paint to buy.

The Maui Historic Commission has published a stylebook for Lahaina, but Lahaina is really no style. Lahaina is just ''as it was'' when the tourists began arriving. The town represents no particular historical period, neither 1850 whaling days nor 1920 plantation days, but just as it was when a retired Amfac plantation manager during the mid-sixties, Keith Tester, said it would be best if Lahaina stayed the way it is, caught between the old and the new. Lahaina is a delightful hodgepodge of architectural styles, beginning with the almost 150-year-old Baldwin House, oldest on Maui, the result of missionaries providing for themselves using the materials available, trying to make it like home. Most of the older buildings were long ago consumed by termites or just disappeared; mostly 1910-1930 buildings have survived. Just not enough time has passed for them to go.

Lahaina has a sort of wild West look about it, as though the posse on horseback would return at any moment if traffic permitted. Parts of Lahaina have been described as looking like Virginia City in Nevada. What it definitely doesn't look like is an old New England town. Neither does it look like an old Hawaii whaling port, except for possibly a hundred feet or so in front of the Pioneer Inn where the restored sailing ship *Carthaginian* is tied up.

Yachting people hanging around the Lahaina Yacht Club bar, those familair with Tahiti, say that, from offshore in the afternoon about a mile out, Lahaina looks exactly like the waterfront of Papeete before the French destroyed the view with fill for wharves dredged up from the harbor bottom. But Lahaina has no Quinn's Bar (even Papeete's has burned down), and is tame for a seaport town. Nothing much has happened since the whaling fleets left, except for a few brief spurts of vitality during the Whaling Spree Festival of twenty years ago (part of the reason why the main stairway in Pioneer Inn leans). Toss down a draft Primo beer in the 100-year-old bar as the late afternoon sun enters the smoky room a few minutes before sunset—a good time and place to drift backward to another time when tourists were sailors off whaling ships.

Lahaina's waterfront shopping street begins at the Banyan Inn, across from the largest banyan tree in the state, and moves northward in and out of carpenter-built falsefronts and elaborate architect-designed emporiums. The people spaces are filled with bare midriffs and halter tops, long white pants, and shirts open to the third button. It is a stroll along many storefronts of jewelry, seashells from everywhere else, and an even half-dozen of very credible restaurants. Some might call the town a bazaar of the bizarre, where the enjoyment of a visit is derived mostly from looking and sharing the experience of being there. From where things begin at Banyan Inn up to the end of the action at the Broiler and back to the Pioneer Inn is a tourist walkway that undoubtedly is enjoyed because it's all real Maui. Mainland entrepreneurs have been unable to erase the sleepy seaport image.

The old Lahaina, before tourists arrived, was very much a town of mom-and-pop stores, some having been in the same family for generations; but their college-educated children had no desire to be store clerks. The plain store fronts selling fishing supplies, oriental foods, hardware, and groceries gradually disappeared as nearby shopping centers drew their customers away and replacement tourists demonstrated little interest in soy sauce and lotus root. Three or four remain on Front Street: Yoshimura Jewelry, the Hop Loo Kazuwara family grocery, George Takauehi, and a small oriental fast-food shop emitting cooking smells that must be quite bewildering to sightseeing tourists. None of what they sell is on hotel menus.

There was a Chinese ice-cream store on the corner where the old men played hanafuda cards all day long, and the barber shop where dropping in and talking was a normal activity. And Freddie's shave ice for the kids. Twenty years ago almost every business up and down Front Street was a locally run business. The local people today are uninterested in selling curios and beach mats to the tourists because the high rents charged by local landlords make it necessary to "go after the buck," as they say. The old store people in their mom-and-pop shops had a different attitude. Running a store was not to make money, but to earn a living. The local people lived for their stores; they enjoyed going to work for the simple pleasure of opening their store in the morning to meet friends and share the day with those who passed by. When a customer came in it was a nice extra.

Small shopkeepers were generally older oriental couples, often an elderly husband retired from the plantation, providing a comfortable cultural bridge from yesterday. They are remembered with a certain nostalgia, and as they closed up shop and left over the years, a distinctive flavor of small-town island life was forever lost. Guzman, the barber, is gone, as is the little store run by Freddie and Mrs. Yamamoto, a fishing supply store stocked with faded boxes of hooks and sinkers, fishing line and flashlights, a barrel filled with bamboo poles, and ice chests to carry beer. Directly in the middle of the store was the most beautiful shave ice machine on Maui, presided over by Freddie with considerable flair. On the left side was a lunch counter with leatherette stools—and Mrs. Yamamoto, maker of the best hamburgers on West Maui (47¢ in 1976), milk shakes with real milk, and steaming hot bowls of her own saimin. It was a popular meeting place for neighborhood kids, and a favorite of local fishermen who hung around for hours to "talk story" with Freddie. Yamamoto's rent kept rising until it was no longer possible for him to keep the store. It was closed and Freddie moved his fishing supplies into the garage at home, where he tried to continue selling fishing supplies. But it was not the same as the busy store had been on Front Street. He died shortly after.

Home-style foods are still available, but it takes a little looking and some traveling to find them all. Most famous are probably Maui's Kitch 'n Cook'd potato chips, a big, thick, old-fashioned chip cooked in oil by the same Kahului family who started packaging the brand many years ago. Maui also excels in Japanese fish cake made of swordfish, and pastries of sweet beans encased in soft dough, Home Maid's crispy manju with a pie crust covering, and Sam Sato and Shishido's mochi. An unusual sherbet called Guri-Guri, probably an old mispronunciation of goody-goody, is packed with sweet beans on request. Tasaka's Candy Store in the Maui Mall Shopping Center

Honolulu photographer Ray Jerome Baker, on a trip to Lahaina about 1910, saw Front Street without any traffic, looking east from the Lahainaluna intersection. Seventy years ago, Lahaina was isolated from the rest of Maui Island—far from Kahului via a winding, cliff-hung road seldom traveled by residents. Lahaina had better connections with Honolulu, using its own direct scheduled steamship service.

makes it, and will pack it to last two-and-a-half hours if you live in Lahaina or Wailea. Maui people know hot dogs are not all alike, that Akahi's are special, along with their Na Ka Oi Portuguese sausage when the batch is spicy hot. Sakuraboshi (dried fish) marinated in shoyu sauce is another island favorite. In season there are fresh Kula persimmons, Lahaina mangoes, Hana guavas, papayas, and breadfruit, Kaupo Gap thimbleberries, and mild Maui onions. All year long there is delightfully dry pineapple wine and pineapple champagne from the Tedeschi winery in 'Ulupalakua—Maui Blanc and Maui Brut. Pause at Bullock's above the Pukalani-Makawao road junction for their marvelous Moonburger, devised when the first astronaut walked on the moon—it was during lunchtime on Maui.

On a return flight from Kaua'i island the baggage will surely contain macadamia nut cookies from the Tip Top Restaurant in Lihu'e, and in spring, sacks full of juicy, wild Koke'e plum. From Hilo there will be Amano fish cake, saloon pilot and cream crackers from Hilo Macaroni Factory, and hot Korean kim chee from Kohala. On Moloka'i is Kanemitsu's small bakery on the main street of Kaunakakai, where in the morning (it may be all gone by noon), enthusiasts buy her delicious Portuguese sweet bread and ''Kanemitsu's Genuine Moloka'i French Bread.'' And from Lani'i island? Juicy pineapples, of course.

Doing its best to keep alive some of the old traditions brought to Hawaii by immigrants from every continent and resting comfortably upon a resilient Hawaiian culture, is the Lahaina Restoration Foundation, a privately financed historical society dedicated to preserving the old. James Luckey, foundation manager, is constantly trying to move backward, building old ships and restoring old buildings to retain for Lahaina some of the special connections with our history and traditions. He is well aware of the futility involved in trying to stop the clock; but talking with Luckey in his 150-year-old office, the old Master's Reading Room for sailing captains, I had the definite impression he would have enjoyed living in another time.

He speaks warmly, with articulate understanding of the foundation's work in restoring their sailing ship, the *Carthaginian*, anchored almost within sight of his office window. Not many people are building sailing ships these days and skilled craftsmen capable of assembling a full-rigged ship are scarce. But to Luckey, it's just a matter of need. In Lahaina, what is needed will sooner or later materialize. Lahaina seems to be that kind of place where just about anybody eventually arrives, the place where dissatisfied people, looking for a better life, find the knob for their hat—the place for their unique skills. Businessmen on the lookout for profitable opportunities, a California restaurant operator wanting to sell his own special way to cook dinner, the catamaran captain eager to carry sightseeing tourists, even the carpenter with a special knack for making things out of wood—these are the people who have always come to Hawaii to stay, and make their own individual contribution. It's been going on for a long time and it continues.

Luckey tells of the day that Van Hope and Patty Langley sailed into Lahaina Harbor in their home-built sailboat, stepped onto the pier, and walked over to admire the *Carthaginian*. They said, We like the looks of your ship, and Jim said, I sure like the looks of yours, too, and they've been in Lahaina ever since, putting the *Carthaginian* together, supervising fabrication and erection of all the rigging, way out here in the middle of the Pacific Ocean.

"Another case," Luckey relates, "was when we wanted to restore the Seaman's Hospital, the old stone building, like others here built with two-foot-thick walls. We found the local skills for making those rock walls was gone. No longer around. But who should be on our gardening crew just arrived from Tonga, but four men, really primitive Polynesians when compared to Hawaii, who are rock workers. Here they are and they're going to work for us. We're going to have Polynesians rebuilding this building!"

The Seaman's Hospital is one of Lahaina's many old buildings, some in ruins, with fascinating stories in their history. It was built by King Kamehameha III in 1836, with a Hawaiian warrior buried in the northeast corner. The king used the house as a sort of out-of-town retreat to get away from Ka'ahumanu, the queen regent, who preferred socializing with the missionaries. He wanted his rum, poker, and a place to entertain girl friends. His sister, Princess Hahiena'ena, was one of the tragic figures of Hawaiian history, caught between the ancient and modern world. She devoutly worshipped the new Protestant God, while still feeling the need to obey the old traditions that would permit her to have a child by her brother, Kamehameha III, to preserve the purity of the royal family. A son by the king and princess was born in 1836, but lived only a few hours, and Hahiena'ena herself died two months later. Along the route of her burial place in Lahaina a path was opened through groves of breadfruit and koa trees, which in later years became known as Luakini Street, the Hawaii word for sacrificial heiau.

Kamehameha's house became the Seamen's Hospital in 1842, then a girls' school in 1860. As one of several Seamen's Hospitals in foreign countries, it was the forerunner of the U.S. Public Health Service, and may have generated the service's first scandal. The last doctor to run the hospital, a man the Rev. Dwight Baldwin didn't think was much of a doctor, was accused of defrauding the government by padding his expense account two dollars a day for over 200 patients in a hospital with beds for less than 100. Records showed patients on the hospital rolls who died the year before. Washington, D.C., sent out a team of investigators who held hearings, collected all the records, and together with witnesses sailed for San Francisco. The ship was never heard from again—it sank with all hands.

Between the incredible and the mundane is the Lahaina that visiting yachts-people from California and Honolulu discovered long ago as an ideal anchorage for three-day weekends or three months. The Lahaina Yacht Club, without boats or harbor, provides an informal gathering place for many Honolulu residents, who make up a large part of the membership. Guests as well as spouses are allowed at the bar and outside dining room, but Lahaina's free lifestyle has forced the membership committee to restrict members to no more than one "spouse" a year.

Private pilots also frequented the yacht club in past years, when Amfac's Ka'anapali Airfield allowed general aviation aircraft to land and park. Only forty minutes from Honolulu in a single-engine Cessna, the strip made Lahaina a pleasant alternative to overcrowded Waikiki for a three-day weekend, golf, or lunch. One morning I landed on the short and narrow Ka'anapali strip after a military version of the DC-3 twin-engined transport had landed, caught its wings in the tall sugarcane growing along each side of the runway, and slid to a stop in the canefield. At the small terminal building office stood the U.S. Marine Corps commanding general berating his pilot for not being aware that the clear distance between the high sugar cane was less than his plane's wingspan. It must have ruined his golf game.

On another occasion it was the U.S. Navy's turn to be embarrassed when on a practice bombing run over nearby Kaho'olawe Island they inexplicably missed the island and dropped a 500-pound bomb on Maui, across the channel and several miles off target. Maui mayor at the time, Elmer Cravalho, had been speaking critically of the navy for months, demanding that it stop the bombing of Kaho'olawe and go somewhere else. He wanted the island returned to Maui County. The navy's position was hardly enhanced when it learned the bomb had actually fallen in the mayor's leased cow pasture just off the road to Lahaina. The navy has been using Kaho'olawe as a gunnery target for warships and a bombing range for carrier aircraft since before World War II, and it was not about to give up the island considered to be of prime importance in maintaining its Pacific fleet's combat readiness. Their spokesman claimed there was not another target island in the entire Pacific Ocean as good and as convenient as Kaho'olawe.

The island is off-limits to everyone; aircraft cannot fly over, fishermen cannot fish close to shore, hunters cannot shoot the thousands of wild goats overgrazing the island. Trespassing is absolutely forbidden. After the mayor, environmental organizations, and antiwar groups took their turns harassing the navy, without forcing any change in the status of Kaho'olawe, the island was "invaded" by a group of Hawaii native political activists claiming the island belonged to the Hawaii people. Their impromptu "navy" was a fleet of small fishing boats mobilized on Maui by supporting friends who intended to bring in food and water as needed. Navy brass took a very dim view of the proceedings, assigned a Marine helicopter to remove the occupation forces and put the leaders in jail.

Native Americans everywhere have become restless—American Indians, Eskimos, and in recent years, the Hawaii people. The goal of Hawaii activists is not too clear; yes, they want the islands returned, claiming that American sugar planters overthrew the Hawaiian kingdom with the connivance of U.S. Marines who happened to be on a ship in Honolulu harbor. Some want to do what is necessary to restore pride in being a Hawaiian; others want to revive old religions and traditions of ancient days, even restore the Hawaiian monarchy. It all may be a quite impractical yearning, but the growth and influence of the Hawaiian 'Ohana (family), politically active organizations, has frightened Hawaiian congressmen and senators into introducing legislation calling for an investigative commission to determine the validity of native claims. Hawaii activists have noted the considerable benefits obtained by Alaska natives and they want to share in the federal largess. Hawaiians have asked for $100 million, or the islands back.

The movement has clearly fostered a Hawaiian cultural renaissance: island music and dance, particularly early chants and ancient hulas in authentic dress, are now seen and heard at numerous public events throughout the year. School children learn Hawaiian hulas, and for the first time since the islands became a U.S. possession, the Hawaiian language, put into written form by the missionaries, is being taught in public schools. Activist leaders say there must be more than just talking, singing, and dancing, that the Hawaiian will never have pride in being Hawaiian without a violent confrontation with the haoles. Older Hawaiians are often embarrassed by all this, native groups appear often to be split by political as well as personality differences, and aggressive tactics by some individuals have frequently proved disastrous.

Legal decisions and political pressure forced the navy to allow Protect Kaho'olawe 'Ohana people onto the island to study village sites and to conduct religious ceremonies. The navy also financed extensive geological and archaeological surveys to locate Hawaiian sites of historical significance. One of the ironies resulting from the navy's bombing of Kaho'olawe and declaration of the island as off-limits is the excellent condition of native historical sites. Archaeologists express pleasure over the unusual opportunity to investigate old sites and fishing shrines undisturbed by artifact collectors or developers' bulldozers—the sites, some hundreds of years old, are still undisturbed, looking as if the Hawaiian fishermen had only recently gotten up and left. The navy's bombing, confined to a small target zone in the center of the island, did not damage any sites. If Kaho'olawe had been open to the public, the sites long ago would have been vandalized and destroyed, as has happened to so many others in Maui County.

When the wind is blowing from the south and the sky is warm, the bombing of Kaho'olawe can sometimes be heard on Maui. White flashes of exploding ordnance are often seen on clear nights, and on occasion even rumbling can be felt like a distant storm. The bombing doesn't do much damage—there's not much damage to be done where for decades the wind has been blowing away the topsoil as fast as the wild goats have eaten the grass growing on top of the island. Perhaps the goats may be the villains—the bombing merely rearranges the dirt a little. On a helicopter visit to the summit target area, to confirm how replanting would survive in a fenced off area (actually quite well), I wandered off by myself to locate the faint bleating of a goat. I followed the sound into a nearby dry gulch where a young goat had caught its foot in an eroded crack. The animal was terribly emaciated and looked barely alive. I broke away the dirt with my boot, and the animal struggled to escape, probably more frightened of me than its predicament. It jumped up, ran a short distance, away from me, and collapsed in the red dust, dead.

A visit to Kaho'olawe with the Kaho'olawe 'Ohana, their older kupanas (elders), young Hawaiians, and camp followers, caught up in the excitement of a new crusade is, at best, a confusing experience to someone standing outside. At Hakioawa Bay, directly across from Wailea and Makena, tents and shelters are scattered in the shade of spindly kiawe growing out of the silt and sand. Around a large table heaped with canned and packaged food supplies are plastic containers of water carried in by boat and helicopter like everything else. It will last for their entire stay, augmented by a dozen different kinds of fish that regularly appear at mealtime. A tremor of excitement passed through the camp when the next day's schedule was discussed—calling for a visit to ancient village sites and shrines, and a hike to the top of the island into the navy's target area accompanied by a military guide. It is as if the participants were on the verge of beginning a great pilgrimage, almost like the first Polynesians exploring their new islands.

Except for several girls with the campers, I was the only haole standing around, an obvious outsider, but the young people eagerly spoke to me, explaining the purpose of their mission on Kaho'olawe: telling me how satisfying it is to discover themselves as Hawaiians, to discover their 'aina (the land), and how important Kaho'olawe is to the Hawaiian "race" and their future. Some conversed in an Hawaiian pidgin I could scarcely understand; all were people who had truly experienced a discovery of themselves and their place in life. They spoke emotionally of "the feeling that is inner peace. To be able to touch the 'aina that has been greatly abused, the purpose that is the same for each and every brother and sister here. It is so beautiful and fulfilling. I've learned so much about the island and her history and I want to be comfortable with the knowledge that someday, in my mo'opuna or my keiki time, she will be respected as she was meant to be . . . . She emits so much power and aloha, that I feel we cannot stop at anything now. We have to press and strive until we accomplish what we set out to do, which is preservation and living out the 'aina. When it is done, maybe others will understand all that has been going on . . . . She has given me so much. The opportunity to do something about what I believe in and the chance to live out my values. The complete aloha between all members of the 'Ohana on Kaho'olawe is really fascinating. There is always warmth and caring among everybody . . . . Knowing that human life is finally on the 'aina which had been barren for decades is overpowering."

The French explorer Jacques Arago, sailing past Kaho'olawe in 1893, noted that "Kaho'olawe will forever be uninhabited because life there is impossible." At night it is cold on Kaho'olawe and the mosquitoes come out. By day proliferating field mice scamper underfoot, climbing table legs in the Hakiowa camp, and crawling inside sleeping bags. The heat is oppressive, the still air hot and humid, characteristic of the island caught in the rain shadow of Haleakala, blocking tradewind weather that would otherwise wet the leached and bare summit landscape. The Kaho'olawe weather has always been like this, with little water available to grow anything except sweet potato and dryland taro—only the fishing is good. Early Hawaiian fishermen established small clusters of huts for temporary stays, and built stone fishing shrines to invoke help from the fish demigod 'Ai'ai, with offerings of leaf and grass bundles filled with tapa, fish bones, pieces of lava rock, and sugarcane stalk. The dryland forest cover of mostly native wiliwili trees was destroyed by a fire that swept the island perhaps 500 years ago, about the time Hawaiians began practicing slash-and-burn agriculture. Since then the descendants of feral goats brought by explorer George Vancouver have overrun the island, effectively preventing recovery of the summit forest, except where kiawe trees fill the narrow gulches. It is doubtful that at any time the island population was much more than 100, even in later years when the island served as a prison for the monarchy.

By decree of the king and chiefs in 1840, the crime of murder was punishable by death, theft and adultery by exile, the men being sent to Kaho'olawe and women to nearby Lana'i on the northwest pali at Lae-o-ka'ena. No food was provided the exiles, and they considered the fish and local yams barely sufficient, so the prisoners made a practice of raiding gardens along the Maui shore in the vicinity of Makena, using stolen outrigger canoes. At times their depredations extended to Ma'alaea and as far as Olawalu, where they stocked up on coconuts and taro before returning to Kaho'oalwe. Having all the food they needed, the men prisoners then went to the exile camp on Lana'i for adulterous women and brought all of them back to Kaho'olawe to share their solitude. The island was made into a very comfortable living place by the exiles, and their continuing daring exploits discouraged the government from molesting them. Everything continued peacefully until 1843, when Kamehameha III put an end to exiling prisoners, a "ridiculous law," as it was called, and sent the exiles to their home islands to work on the roads. It must have been a very disappointing decision to the men and women on Kaho'olawe.

Long before the U.S. Navy converted Kahoʻolawe Island into a bombing target, the summit soil was leached and eroded over hundreds of acres. In this 1916 photograph, a native wiliwili tree has been almost completely undermined by wind erosion, and left stranded with only few roots to hold it in place in the island desert.

Talking with Dr. Emmett Aluli at the Hakioawa camp, I asked him why the Kahoʻolawe ʻOhana perpetuates Kahoʻolawe as a symbol for the Hawaiian renaissance. It seemed a dreadful example to me. Was it just for newspaper headlines? Why not do something to stop tourist development at Makena? Or to halt continuing destruction by grazing cattle and by artifact collectors in the extensive village ruins along the Haleakala shore? As I spoke he gradually walked me away from the ʻOhana members busily preparing lunch, as if he did not want opposing opinions to be heard by others. I was reminded of his reply to my suggestion for establishing a Hawaiian land trust to hold undivided-interest lands in Kipahulu Valley for Hawaiians who would live on the land in "traditional ways." He was not interested in such a compromise. "You overthrew our kingdom and took our lands. We want our land back," he stated. I could offer him nothing; the islands were also mine. I live here, too.

Leaving Aluli and Kahoʻolawe, I was more aware than ever that an eventual confrontation was due. But need there be any guilt feelings or apologies made for the magnificent community we, the people of the United States and recent immigrants from around the world, have created on the islands of Hawaii? I am intrigued by the fact that it was an Hawaiian developer named Aluli who built one of the first condominiums on Maui. Perhaps if the Hawaiian ʻOhana people now camped out on Kahoʻolawe were able to afford living in a Maui condominium there would be less talk of confrontation.

In the commendable efforts of native Hawaiians to achieve a cultural and religious renaissance, there is a danger of losing the great virtues and beauties of the present. There must be something in the Hawaiian living style that has been the catalyst for establishing Hawaii's great amalgam of people, a people not living in separate ethnic neighborhoods or religious parishes but together in a democratic community. It may be true that the native Hawaiian has lost much of his old communal lifestyle and even the ability to survive in a highly competitive society, but the Hawaiian has surely gained considerable more in the process. Samuel Amalu, the *Advertiser* columnist, recalls a number of Samoans living in Honolulu telling him how dumb the Hawaiians were for losing so much of their lands to other races. They reminded Amalu that the Samoans in Samoa still owned their own native lands. So then Amalu asked, "Well and good, but then what are you doing here?"

I fail to understand the logic, if any, of a need for identity with the land—"my land," as tribal people say. The war drums began beating when someone decided they had an identity crisis and took to the courts to resolve the problem. Hawaiian activists decided they had no identity without land and a nation to control it. The search for identity assumed a strange twist when some Hawaiians decided it was perfectly permissible to violate legislatively established law, and when arrested to stand on "constitutional rights" of trial by jury. Others say laws need not be obeyed because American laws are not their laws; and the Christian religion is not a Hawaii religion. And all in the name of schemes to convince vote-scrounging politicians to support claims for unearned money from the federal government. It is all a divisive philosophy and has no place in America, let alone in Hawaii.

Growing up in Hawaii grants a special perspective to living—a place to stand and look at the world without stepping off or dropping out. My sense of being and identity has been realized through an understanding of my own personal, cultural, and spiritual heritage. It is the collective ethos of everything that has happened to date, gained from diverse encounters in countries on every continent, influenced by the environment, and modified by international and national events that forced me to respond. I refuse to accept an identity confining me to a particular ethnic, or cultural group. If we must have an identity, make it one with the earth. We are, where we are, seems sufficient.

From my tent on the Kaho'olawe beach, Maui had a certain fascination at night. The Hawaiians camped a short distance away were attempting to immerse the contemporary environment in ancient motifs. It interferes with living in 1980. Across the channel, automobile headlights suddenly glared then flickered out as they turned a corner somewhere. The lights of hotels and apartments at Wailea were part of another world far away, because the philosophical gap between Kaho'olawe and Wailea is beyond reach. When the helicopter returned me to Wailea in the morning, the flight took only a few minutes for me. It is over a thousand years for the Hawaiian people.

The whirling baggage carousel at Kahului Airport spins off baggage from every island: large boxes and small boxes, bags and sacks, and crowing fighting cocks on weekends. Pie and cake boxes are tucked under the seats and carried out by hand, but an occasional oil-stained shopping bag with potato chips dropping out also ends up with the baggage, alongside brand-name plastic bags and string-tied beer cases stuffed with everything but beer. The aluminum cases and Samsonite bags belong to the tourists. Everything else is local stuff carried inter-island by Hawaii residents who fly more per capita than anyone else in the nation.

On the other populated Maui islands, Lana'i and Moloka'i, the living style is considerably more relaxed. All is smaller and in scale with the fewer number of people, especially on Lana'i, where the only hotel, Hotel Lana'i, has only eleven rooms, and the highway people have deemed it necessary to pave only half the public roads. Lana'i is where the first two cars brought to the island many years ago, the only vehicles on the island at the time, were wiped out in a head-on collision. Considering the small size of the Lana'i community, there is always a lot going on.

Like Hana people objecting to the hordes of tourists crowding the Hana Road in rental Datsuns, the Lana'i people also have their problems with tourists. On Lana'i it is the weekend sailors and tour boat operators bringing day-trip visitors from Lahaina to the only swimming beach on Lana'i at Hulopoe Bay. All week long yacht-people would anchor in the beautiful bay, defecate in the clear waters, and throw their garbage overboard. On weekends, the only days Lana'i pineapple workers had off to take their families to their only beach, picnic tables, surf, and the beach itself would sometimes be monopolized by a hundred visitors from Lahaina, unaware of the ill feeling their seemingly innocent day at the beach was provoking. Boats are now banned from the bay, and tour boat operators have agreed to never carry tourists to Lana'i on Sunday.

Never-on-Sunday has a special significance on Lana'i, and may also be a warning to the growing tourist industry about the increasing conflicts with island residents. On Lana'i the once academic question of how many tourists is too many has already been answered. Many residents of Hana now want to blockade their famed road. Increasing friction between visitors and young islanders may be not so much a matter of delinquency as a manifestation of feeling that they are being crowded off their island, and forced to work in hotels instead of fishing and shooting wild pig. When Sheraton opened its new Moloka'i hotel, a Hawaii activist group calling itself Hui Alaloa demonstrated in the hotel's parking lot, objecting to the development. Walter Ritte, organizer of the protest, explained, "My search for my identity as a Hawaiian and for the Hawaiian culture is paramount. The economics of Moloka'i come second. I know we can live off the land and the ocean like our forefathers."

It is doubtful that Moloka'i people staffing the new hotel support this philosophy: few Hawaiians would give up their car and TV in exchange for a canoe and taro patch. As the economic contours of the island change, so will the cultural attitudes and lifestyles. The antitourist advocates will always be a minority, albeit a noisy one—there are too many Hawaiian tour bus drivers earning a good living from tourism. But residents find it very uncomfortable dragging their hibachis, coolers, and the kids and aunties through hotel lobbies to the rich haole beach preserves. The awkward situation demands an early solution, as does the preservation of Hawaii's fragile scenic resources.

Lars-Eric Lindblad's famed cruise ship, *Lindblad Explorer*, has been taking visitors to some of the more remote reaches of the Pacific for over ten years, and his concern for the Pacific's cultural heritage has grown with these years. He now feels the Pacific needs urgent attention. "Having robbed the people of O'ahu of Waikiki, after having destroyed a heritage which they had no right to destroy," says Lindblad, "the exploiters are now turning to the other islands, Maui being most threatened at the moment. As we conserve our wildlife and our wilderness, we have to conserve these islands which have a natural beauty unparalleled in the rest of the United States. It can be done and it must be done."

It was the first day of the third annual Halawa Fishing Tournament, and at first glance, when we turned down the winding road into Halawa Valley, it looked like every campsite was already taken. A kaleidoscope of color covered Halawa Beach, from huge olive-drab army surplus tents to odd spots of bright green, yellow, and blue shapes of synthetic fiber, and palm fronds woven into thatched windbreaks protected well-trampled grass campsites of people who had been there for several days. We were late arrivals, but did find space between the fishermen to pitch our tents before a steady drizzle set in for the night, eating dinner with the rain spattering loudly into our Sierra Club cups. We climbed into our sleeping bags early, to be up at first light, for departure to Wailau Valley by boat the next morning, the first stop on a week's trip into every valley on the Moloka'i north shore. There were nine of us, five women and four men, all having been told that each afternoon we would be swimming ashore to our campsite.

Twin outboard-powered fishing boats churned in and out of the bay all morning as we waited our turn to load up. A high surf was running, with waves breaking completely across the entrance to Halawa Bay, forcing outgoing boats to carefully watch the breaking sets, waiting until the third and fourth waves before suddenly accelerating straight into the oncoming surge. When their judgment was correct, the wave did not break but flattened out as the boat sped safely into the open sea. Incoming boats wallowed slowly on the smooth beach behind breaking waves, motors idling, until the boatman, standing up to look over the waves, saw the right combination and, with the skill of a professional, quickly charged forward at full throttle, pushing the boat through the top of the wave to coast down into the bottom and surf shoreward. It looked easy when done correctly, but it was with some trepidation that we waded out to our boat and climbed aboard to ride the surf ourselves. Our boatman, Hawaiian Jules Duduoit, scion of an old Moloka'i family, welcomed us aboard.

Springing loose into the rough seas outside Halawa, we traveled westward about a quarter mile from shore. To people on the flat leeward side of Moloka'i, we were "behind" on the north shore behind the mountain backbone of Moloka'i. We were where the cliffs rise straight from the ocean, with no reef to soften the waves breaking directly against the vertical rock cliff, where the surging blue ocean dissolves into white froth along the bottom of the pali, like a black wolfhound breaking into a broad grin. Interrupted only by narrow valleys, the sea cliff rises to 3,000 feet above the sea, where the misty tops penetrate low-hanging clouds, draining them of rain that clings to the cliff like a curtain of wet strings. Between Wailau and Pelekunu the sea cliff is said to be the highest in the world. Even more than Napali on Kaua'i, this may be the last Hawaii wilderness.

Shortly before Papalaua Valley is Pipiwai. It means sprinkling water, aptly descriptive of a tiny stream falling down the cliff, on some days blown completely away by the wind into a spray that disappears in the air. Several years ago we walked into Papalaua, rock-hopping at the base of the cliff, intending to return by the same route. We were prepared for the worst and the worst happened when long swells appeared offshore, smashing giant waves against the pali. Trying to pass under the sea arch at Keanapuka we were swept off the slippery rocks and only by getting caught between them were we saved from being swept into the surf. We climbed out a little chastened and camped for the night without traveling farther.

Seas were still high in the morning, making the choice of how to get out limited to only one—straight up. We carried the necessary pitons and rope, and began the climb, camping the first night on a rocky ledge only wide enough for our tent, but with wild taro and running water—actually, a very satisfactory camp site, if a trifle narrow. We were about 500 feet up the cliff and felt confident of being able to climb the remaining 1,300 feet before dark the next day; but firm rock soon disappeared, making it necessary to anchor our rope around at least six pitons in the unstable lava. When everyone was secure, one of us tugged on the rope, jerking out each piton one by one to recover them for use on the next short climb. At dusk we were still climbing vertically, so each of us squirmed carefully into sleeping bags, secured everything in a rope net, and literally spiked ourselves to the cliff for the night. I remember sleeping soundly—not tossing at all. We climbed out the next day without incident, walked back to our car parked in Halawa, and arrived at the airport in time for the afternoon plane. We were a day late in returning the rental car, so the owners had notified the police who found the locked car but not us; so they left the car, assuming correctly that we would be out sooner or later unless we had drowned.

It apparently is the demeanor of Moloka'i police to not get too excited. I rented a vacation house at Waialua, about as far as you can get from Kaunakakai, and found posted on the kitchen wall the usual instructions for renters, plus several comments found only on Moloka'i: "If the house catches fire, gather your valuables and go outside. The fire department will not arrive in time to do any good." And then, "The Moloka'i police never come this far except in case of murder."

A very exclusive campsite, 500 feet up the Moloka'i pali between Halawa and Papalaua Valleys. Wide enough to pitch a tent, the cliffside campsite provided wild taro, a freshwater spring, and a magnificent unobstructed view of the Pacific Ocean.

Nearing Wailau Valley, our camp for the night, we moved closer inshore where we looked overhead to see the waterfalls fall out of the sky. When we turned the corner into Wailau cove the ocean was suddenly calm, and water sliding down the cliff face slipped quietly into the sea. At first we saw no sign of life on the beach and were momentarily elated over the possibility of having the valley to ourselves. We moved closer. The beach was still empty, but then, at the last place where camping was possible, three blue tents were seen behind bluish campfire smoke curling into the air. We wouldn't be alone, but then being alone even on Moloka'i is hardly possible anymore.

Just as we were becoming adjusted to having fellow campers with us on the beach, a helicopter fluttered earthward across the valley, dropping off other visitors. It was very disturbing, its presence seeming to spoil the valley and our good feeling; I wondered about the incident and my apparent desire to have the wilderness just for us. It was so pleasant until these strangers, these interlopers, showed up. They were not one of us—therefore they didn't belong. Is wilderness really that elitist, in that it must be exclusive? Or was it the noisy helicopter that so seriously intruded upon my pleasure? The helicopter flew away, and the valley became quiet again—ours again. Our boatman tossed the anchor overboard. We could swim from here.

We inflated an inner tube to carry our gear, stacked it high, and jumped feet first into the cold water. My toes touched the sandy bottom at the same time water reached my neck, and I started swimming for the beach about fifty yards away, pushing the inner tube ahead. Carefully watching the surf so our gear would not be tossed over and drenched, we picked up the tube upon reaching shallow water and ran it up beyond the reach of the waves. After three round trips we had everything ashore. Jules returned in his boat to Halawa while we carried our gear past the blue tents toward a suitable open space near where Wailau Stream entered the ocean. On this side of the island the sun sets early, so it was dark by the time we prepared dinner. The ocean became black and stars took over the sky. Far away on the horizon, the lighthouse at Kalaupapa settlement flashed its coded light, giving a limit to the featureless space. We were soon asleep.

In the morning we met our fellow campers. Adding us, the population of Wailau was now exactly thirty-two, not all transients, as we soon learned. Behind and a little above the blue-tent Hawaiian colony, which was perched on a small ledge, was an attractive hut constructed entirely of bamboo. Clear plastic sheeting covered the roof and walls, except for the one open side facing onto the beach and ocean, providing a grand view out and in. We could see into every part of the informal house and the occupants welcomed our interest. It seemed a very practical living place on a beautiful site that would be the envy of anyone in expensive Ka'anapali. Here it was free for the time taken to build it. The builders told of flying past Moloka'i on the way to Maui and of admiring the beautiful valley, and without much debate decided it was a good place to live; they built the house of bamboo they cut themselves. The husband takes odd jobs outside, sufficient to buy food, then quits and returns to Wailau until they need more food. "Living in Wailau costs only food," they said, as I watched their young daughter squeeze juice from wild passion fruit. I was incredulous that in our complex and dependent society it was still possible to escape into an Arcadian world. I asked about the young friend of their daughter and was told her mother was walking in on the Wailau trail, across the island from the other side. They expected her in a week or so. It was another intriguing aspect of Wailau that we quickly learned to appreciate: a "week" is a short enough measure for time. I took off my wristwatch.

Further inside Wailau, under the java plum forest was another settler with a bamboo house: a thin, bearded young man, who slept on the floor and dressed in ragged pants without any shirt. He talked little about himself, but the Hawaiian families camped in the blue tents filled in the gaps. He arrived about a year ago, they said, overweight by at least 200 pounds. His wife and children had left him, and after learning about Wailau he came here to forget and start over. He has no money, they said, mooches a lot, and barters his personal things for food, not wanting to venture outside and work. He traded his binoculars for five pounds of rice, asking if they had brown rice when they gave him white. He next wanted to trade his compass for more rice, but the Hawaiians didn't need a compass. He was having a difficult time and was not expected to be around very long. For some, Wailau is not an escape.

The Hawaiian families camped in the blue plastic shelters moved into Wailau every spring, as soon as winter waves subsided. They stayed for the summer, occasionally returning by boat to meet friends at Halawa bringing supplies of food and beer. Wailau Valley was a summer home in the old Hawaiian style, and they have returned every year since they were little children, the men arranging their outside work to conform to a winter schedule and the women hoping they become pregnant in the spring so they would give birth outside in the winter. One father was a school bus driver, which seemed an ideal occupation for people whose beach parties last all summer.

They were a gregarious group, relaxed and friendly in a disarming way. After five minutes I felt like I, too, had been returning again and again on these summer picnics. Their large beer cooler was bottomless and during the hot midday became the most used item in camp. On the rocky beach we shared beer, crab, and poi, the small, soft crab requiring much sucking on the legs to get the meat out, then sucking on our fingers to get the poi off, and drinking beer to wash it all down. It was a most satisfying lunch.

Guitars and ukuleles were taken from the shelter in late afternoon after shadows cast by the pali had cooled the best large rocks for sitting on. ''Mokuleia'' was strummed without words and other music was improvised around the fire as everyone took their turn on a ukulele. A Hawaiian woman picked up her ukulele and softly sang, ''. . . a beautiful island across the sea—beautiful Hawaii.'' It was magic. Some were drinking beer, looking at the fire. Others gathered around a deck of cards, carefully balancing half-empty beer cans on the round beach rocks. A boy and girl crawled into the tent and kissed quietly while the last color of the setting sun faded away, with the brightening Kalaupapa light again casting its coded signal into the night. The surf was suddenly louder, and a fisherman abruptly stood to light his pressure gasoline lamp and inspect the row of bamboo fishing poles wedged in the beach rocks. The shimmering fishing lines disappeared into the darkness, tiny copper cowbells dangling loose on the taut lines. They would tinkle when the fish struck.

We were up early impatiently waiting for Jules Dudoit and our boat. The ocean was rough, too rough to successfully land our gear on the beach at Pelekunu, so we resigned ourselves to swimming ashore for the day. Jules had not arrived by mid-morning and we became concerned that our boatman would again be late. We had been late leaving Halawa because his two engines wouldn't start, something about the coils burning out, making it necessary for him to drive back into town for a new pair, but the gas stations were all closed and it was necessary to borrow coils from the cars of friends. I had the impression his friends didn't know this yet.

We applauded when Jules finally did appear, gliding smoothly into the bay as he cut the engines to drop anchor. He waved for us to swim out, and we all were soon aboard. Anxious as we were to leave, Jules wanted to pick up another, larger anchor from a nearby boat, which turned out to be quite an involved operation in the tossing waves, what with keeping the boats apart and untangling lines in the open hatch. Finally Jules got everything the way he wanted, started the engines, and we roared out to meet the open ocean swells at full throttle.

Like all powerboat people, Jules knows only two speeds—stop or top speed forward. We slammed into every wave with a solid thud and were airborne off the crest of the biggest. I was thinking of asking him to slow down, when I noticed the tachometer needle for the portside engine slowly moving backward on the dial. It stopped at zero. Jules reached for the ignition key and turned it off. As the boat slowed to one-motor speed, it gradually climbed the backside of an ocean swell, came almost to a halt at the top, then slid beautifully down the far side. Jules unhooked the engine hatch and began tinkering and fiddling while we watched the rocks along the shore. After exhausting his supply of tools, the engine resumed a normal roar and we started slamming into the waves again at top speed. I felt it better not to ask him to slow down.

The waves rolling into Pelekunu Bay were as anticipated, breaking into powerful surf far from shore. Only strong swimmers would make it, and it was obvious that it would be impossible to get our camping gear onto the beach in one piece. As we dove off our boat into the churning water, Jules kept the engines running without dropping anchor, and pulled immediately away when the last person was over the side. I saw a Hawaiian hurrying down the Pelekunu Beach toward our landing place, naked except for shorts, with a dog and two small children following. We were to receive a welcome quite different from Wailau.

Walter Ritte, leader of Moloka'i Hawaiian activist groups, approached us belligerently as we greeted him. He offered no aloha. ''Who's in charge?''
''We all are.''
''What are you here for?'' he growled.
''Sightseeing.''
''How long are you here for?''
''Just today. Maybe noon. What's the matter. Isn't this public property?''
''Yes, the beach is public, but beyond is private.'' He gestured inland, saying, ''Don't go toward that house.''
''Whose land is it?''

"Lots of people. We're trying to protect the valley for lots of people, Hawaiians. If you're going to make any monies on this trip in Pelekunu, going to write a book or something, the royalties go to the valley. I recommend you stay away from over there," and he pointed to a blue plastic covered house. "Those people aren't very friendly." He turned and walked away without saying more.

Walter Ritte's handmade house in Pelekunu is another basic bamboo structure, with partially thatched roof and walls of woven dry pandanus leaves. The roof is made water-tight against frequent afternoon rains with the familiar blue plastic, and true to his principles, at the front entrance is posted a sign, "No tourist allowed." Ritte means what he says about Pelekunu Valley. "We are going to keep tourists out of here. If we have to, we'll use guns. This is our last stand. I consider my back against the wall."

With his wife, Loretta, a former Miss Hawaii, Ritte and three other Hawaiian families have withdrawn from the eight-hour day and moved to the Moloka'i north shore, where each built a small house, planted taro and other crops, fish the plentiful ocean, and hunt wild boar and goats. Ritte describes the experience as learning as much as he can about himself; "I must get back to the land. We have a phrase: Aloha 'aina—Love of the land! It's what took me to Kaho'olawe, and it's what brought me here."

On our return to Wailau, Jules stopped for spear fishing around the rock islands, and we waded ashore at camp carrying po'opu, manini, and uhu, to share with everyone. I explained how easy it was to catch baby goat by running them down on foot, but there were no volunteers for running. Young goat makes a tasty meal marinated in hot spices and broiled over kiawe charcoal. Our crew possessed all the skill necessary to use the squirming things picked up along the shore: potato salad with Wailau lobster and crab, hotcakes with thimbleberry jam and wild lilikoi (passion fruit) syrup, fresh watercress from Wailau Stream, opihi shellfish, and fragrant yellow and white ginger flowers on the table rocks. Guava squeezed through someone's ventilated tennis hat became guava jelly; we found bamboo shoots, and cooked green papaya into a tasty squash; freshwater crawfish fried in a mixture of Bisquick and beer became classic Japanese shrimp tempura; and lilikoi pulp squeezed into juice and combined with rum and crushed ice from the beer cooler made a fantastic daiquiri. (For crushed ice we filled a towel with ice, placed it on top of a rock, and reduced the ice chunks to crushed ice by hammering the towel with another rock.) I have wondered ever since if it would have been possible to stay in Wailau for very long before they invented insulated coolers.

Our Hawaiian friends had brought in a turkey for dinner, roasting it on a turning spit, and I made notes on what was required: one, a pile of puka-puka lava rock in a circle about eighteen inches high to hold the charcoal, support the spit and contain the heat; two, a spit for the turkey made of a one-inch diameter green guava branch cut from a tree shaped like a handle for turning; three, a fire to heat the rocks and make an ash base; four, a second fire built nearby to produce additional charcoal as needed; five, the turkey wrapped in aluminum foil and wired to the spit; six, a portable radio to receive Hawaiian music from Honolulu; and seven, probably the most important, at least six cans of beer per spit-turner per pound of turkey; a fifteen-pound turkey requiring at least fifteen six-packs of beer to roast.

At breakfast our camp was in shade, and we guessed the time of day by the shadow edge on the opposite wall of Wailau Valley as it crept slowly downward, like a giant sun-dial. With the sun behind us breakfast was always in the cool shade, lunch was out somewhere on the trail or along the beach, and in the late afternoon we would begin preparations for dinner when the sun was three outstretched fingers above the horizon. Started then it would be twilight when we finished dessert and dark after coffee. Fresh water was in Wailau Stream twenty feet from our tents, conveniently located for dishwashing and to provide lulling water harmonics at night when the stream asserted its own swishing sound heard between wave sets when the ocean surf was quiet.

We moved over to Papalaua Valley for our last days on Moloka'i, saying a fond good-bye to our Hawaiian friends before swimming out to Jules' boat. The day was beautiful with a scattering of wispy clouds reflected on the calm ocean, barely rippled by a slight breeze. Past Kikipau Point we caught our first glimpse of our destination—water falling from the sky in a narrow 2,000-foot-long slot far back inside Papalaua Valley. Our new campsite was straight ahead on the opposite shore where we could see hardly a ripple of white surf. We clambered over the side into transparent water, clean and clear, at exactly the correct temperature for swimming. No other tents could be seen.

For two days we would have Papalaua Valley for ourselves—our valley. I'm sure I would have been deeply resentful if anyone else came ashore to camp nearby and disturb our exclusive place. As it was, I was quite disturbed by a helicopter load of tourists that came by to hover over our camp, as if they were counting how many people were in Papalaua that night. I guess everyone needs a valley of their own.

When I heard the plopping of helicopter blades again, I became angry. Why must these people disturb us? The helicopter came in low this time, directly over our camp, and I was ready to shake my fist at it, when I recognized the *Kiele*, belonging to Chris Hemmeter, builder of the new Hyatt Regency Maui Hotel at Ka'anapali. A box was slowly lowered from the open door and several of us ran to grab it before the contents spilled. The rope holding it dropped free and the helicopter heeled over in a graceful arc and flew off. We opened the box quickly, finding inside fifteen T-bone steaks, four bottles of chilled wine, an assortment of cheese, a box of chocolate-coated macadamia nuts and one watermelon. If we were to be alone on this isolated beach, I guess this was the best way, with a treasure chest delivered by helicopter! We placed the watermelon carefully beneath the nearby waterfall to keep it cold until after dinner and rearranged the contents of our cooler to accommodate the steaks and chocolate nuts. As an environmentalist I should be critical of the helicopter intruding upon our quiet valley, but I enjoyed the steaks and watermelon anyway.

Our last breakfast: a stir-fried mix of bits and pieces remaining in the cooler. Last-minute collections of opihi were packed in ice to carry out, and we waited for our last wade into the ocean with our thoughts of a week on the Hawaiian land—our own aloha 'aina; the good friends in Wailau and the antagonism in Pelekunu. We finished eating and threw our plastic forks and spoons into the fire. We had washed them after every meal for a week, now we were rid of them. It seemed a final symbolic act. In some ways we were glad to not be sitting on hard rocks anymore—all the places to sit had been used. My bottom was numb and my feet sore from walking on round rocks. We packed our gear and waited for the boat.

Our last day on the north shore of Moloka'i. It begins to rain, appropriately for a sad day, with only a little blue showing between the broken overcast to let us know the sky was still there. The surf was up a bit from yesterday; must be a general storm in the area. On rainy tradewind days only the mountains will be shaded by clouds, but today as far as we could see toward the horizon it was overcast. The waterfalls were running full, the island overflowing from the night's rain, and the air was cool and pleasant. In some ways I hoped that Jules and his boat would not show. Perhaps the engine would fail again. What if he never returned to pick us up?

It was good to learn what time really is. To be where any time within a week was good enough; where the day began at dawn and ended at dusk. We ate at the beginning and end of daylight and bathed in cold Wailau Stream when it was hot. Nothing was done because it was time to be done, yet everything happened because it was the right time. I shall always remember the light rainshowers drifting out of Wailau Valley in the afternoon; cold drops blowing against my face from the gray mist. And the night sky of stars never seen in the city, with dark cloud shapes blowing by on the wind.

I had wanted to interview the Hawaiian people in Wailau and take their photographs, but could not bring myself to even ask, knowing it would have invaded their privacy. I did not even ask their names. It was nice to have shared their blue shelter on that beautiful evening with the guitars, soft Hawaiian music, poi, cracked crab, and beer. But it was always ''them and us'' and I could not help feeling that I was the intruder into ''their valley.'' Yet, their aloha and hospitality was not just polite, but sincere and genuine. It could not be overlooked, however, that Wailau was crowded that night and we were, perhaps, the nine that made it too many.

How can I hope that those who read this will not visit Wailau? That photographs of the Moloka'i I love will not be the instruments of destruction? But how can we save the places we love unless the people outside know it is worth saving? Wailau will not be preserved as the isolated valley it is now by keeping the valley secret, or by not praising its beauty. We must know the valley if we are to save Wailau and all other Maui valleys.

On that beautiful night when we shared poi and ukeleles, an elderly Hawaiian woman saw me taking notes. She was born in Wailau. She spoke to me softly, saying, ''Please don't write about Wailau.'' □

Always hovering in the distance, low on the horizon, Kaho'olawe Island ⊏⟩ is the navy's bombing target and a native Hawaii political symbol in the struggle to ''get back our land.'' Kaho'olawe is the only Maui island without a tour boat or hotels. Uninhabited and littered with unexploded ordnance, naval authorities continue keeping visitors away from what tourist maps call the ''island of death.''

In an unfolding drama, the land and people share an evolving heritage that continues to change and grow without the inhibiting shackles of cultural isolation.

The natural scene contrasts greatly with the carefully manicured environment (overleaf) of trees and plants assembled by landscape architects and gardeners at Wailea. The cinder-pimpled shoulder of Haleakala and flat profile of Kaho'olawe are the only identification with old realities on the new Wailea golf courses and tiger claw trees at Wailea Ekolu village. ⟡

Hasegawa says he does know where everything is in the amply-stocked Hasegawa General Store, including the wine, papaya, rifles, Band-aid, cheese, charcoal, canned fruit, tennis shoes, candy bars, aloha shirts, postcards, cotton yardage, potatoes, magazines, beer, frozen meat, books, the Honolulu and Maui newspapers, towels, paper clips, hammers, gasoline, bacon, and many other items that only Hasegawa knows about.

Ka'anapali Beach (overleaf), the Waikiki of Maui. Amfac created the
popular resort complex on caneland bordering the longest continuous
beach on Maui, a beach that previously had been open only to sugar company employees. Today the famous beach offers fun to thousands each
day. The newest Ka'anapali hotel, the Hyatt Regency Maui, has added
more than 800 rooms to what is quite likely one of the most famous vacation beaches in the world.

Hana children play in the lava cauldrons along the Wai'anapanapa shore,
a rocky maze emulating the indigenous Koa forest tangle in upper Kaupo
Gap at the national park boundary.

From two miles high, directly above Kahoʻolawe Island the military
bombing range is a clear target. The leached, eroded earth is the conse-
quence of a hundred years of overgrazing by cattle and goats on an arid
island where the huge hulk of Haleakala blocks tradewind rains.
Haleakala looms high on Maui, seven miles across ʻAlalakeiki Channel.

Islands by their very nature are finite landscapes, extending from elusive
mountain summits to the sea, and, at times, beyond those limits—above
the tradewind clouds and below the waves, where migrating humpback
whales are annual visitors. Outrigger canoe racers make silver trails in
Lahaina Roads, the historical anchorage between Lanaʻi and Maui.

Virtually impossible to visit, a dangerous place to stroll without a bomb disposal squad walking ahead, Kaho'olawe Island has become a controversial landscape bombed by the military and claimed as sacred land by Hawaii political activists. Ironically, it has been the navy's prohibition against entry that has effectively preserved the many native archeological sites, protecting them from destruction by bulldozers and artifact collectors. Navy bombing targets are miles from abandoned village sites. Archeologists studying the island's historical sites talk excitedly of finding fishing shrines hundreds of years old, looking as if the fishermen had just left, because no one has been ashore to disturb them. Haleakala is a perfect volcanic peak in an unusual view from the Hakioawa Bay shore, directly across the channel from Makena.

Native activists calling themselves the Kahoʻolawe Ohana demand that
Kahoʻolawe be returned to the Hawaii people, although few would want
a return to the old days of Hawaii. Captain Cook saw warriors with gourd

helmets in 1778 when he landed at Kealakekua Bay. Eroded basalt rocks near a Kahoʻolawe village site offer an eerie cantation of decayed temple images, a reminder of the harshness of ancient Hawaii ways.

Papalaua Valley embraces a slender thread of water sliding down a 3,000 foot pali into the never inhabited, seldom visited valley, an aerial landmark for thousands of visitors flying small commuter airlines along the precipitous north shore of Moloka'i.

Mokapu Island, little more than a large rock along the Molokaʻi north shore, where there is no barrier reef to protect the exposed valleys from rough winter seas. Summer is when the fishermen are out and campers pitch their tents on otherwise isolated beaches nearby.

They are the children of Maui, enjoying themselves in cultural festivities
and fully aware of the rich traditions bequeathed to them.

They hardly look like ancient Hawaii inscriptions. A dog on a leash? The enigmatic petroglyphs at Luahiwa on Lana'i also depict, on the incised lichen covered rock, people on horseback, dogs, and cats. A long-deceased Hawaii resident of Lahaina said the old graffiti were made about 1870 by students from Lahainaluna School on a Lana'i vacation.

Shipwreck beach on Lana'i and Wailau Beach on Moloka'i reveal contrasting images of Maui—wasteful human accumulation and nature's pristine beauty. Offshore of Lana'i lies the hulk of an abandoned tanker from World War II. On rocky tideland flats is scattered broken timber from the sailing schooner *Helene Port Townsend,* out of Puget Sound a century ago. Opposite, isolated Wailau Beach still reflects the beauty of a thousand years past.

Isolated Kalaupapa settlement, formerly a dreaded place of banishment for lepers, is now only a mule ride away from the rest of Molokai. Once exiled to Kalaupapa forever, with death their only release, the remaining patients, their disease now arrested and no longer a danger to visitors, stay on in the quiet peninsula community, preferring simple rural lifestyle to the demanding urban commotion outside.

On the hill above Kalaupapa on Moloka'i Island is Kaule o Nanahoa, the phallic rock, a symbol of rebirth and renewal.

◁ Overleaf. Warning signs posted in the vast Kapuaiwa Coconut Grove on Moloka'i warn visitors of falling coconuts, but the view through palm fronds to the sky and across the sparkling leeward sea to Lana'i tempt many to chance a bong on the head.

The random patterns seen from the sky are pineapple fields on Lana'i—some ready for picking, others freshly plowed and ready for planting. Lana'i City forms a different kind of pattern in the upper left corner, and front yards of residents typically present their own individual needs. Bergilio and Lydian Batoon live in a two-bedroom company house on Lana'i Avenue, where they have planted their front yard into a grand mix of virtually everything growable in Hawaii, including a lemon tree, seven varieties of cactus, tree fern, orchids, and banana. Their backyard is a supermarket of vegetables.

Seen from the Munro trail to the summit of Lana'ihale, Kaho'olawe lies
flat on the horizon. Path-like trails on the calm ocean surface are
reminders that this is Kealaikahiki Channel, the traditional "path to
Tahiti," where return voyagers many generations ago set canoes on the
direct route to Tahiti, three thousand miles directly south of Hawaii.
From Palaoa Point, at Kaunolu village site on Lana'i, navigators would
receive a further affirming check on their relationship to the stars. On
Moloka'i Island, above, the beach at Wailau Valley displays a confused
surf washing black volcanic sand.

Kahakuloa Head is an easily identifiable landmark even under the gray skies of an island squall. Rain is as much a part of the Hawaii climate as sun, and while accompanying weather can be violent, temporarily converting sandy beaches into piles of jumbled boulders, the storm soon blows away, leaving streams placidly draining wet valleys. Idyllic environments like Wailau Valley seem little affected by passing storms. Nobody is there to note any changes.

This must be the place. The place people yearn for, and dream of. This must be that place where all of nature's beauty finds focus, to reveal the wonder of the earth. This is my kind of place.